PRAISE FOR C

AN INDIE

"Precise and erudite, Barrera's writing is as alluring and arresting as the landscapes and stories it conveys. Each piece is crafted with care, imbued with Barrera's poignant critical sense and her perspicacious ability to unravel the different levels of affect, historicity, and magnificence that constitute the everyday life of each lighthouse."
    —*LOS ANGELES REVIEW OF BOOKS*

"A dark and often obsessive meditation on what it feels like to squirrel yourself away from the world and embrace isolation in the name of pursuing a passion…something beyond just a good-natured study of shipwrecks and their saviors."
    —*SAN FRANCISCO CHRONICLE*

"The attentive lyricism of [Barrera's] self-exploration pulls the reader steadily along the craggy coastlines of the world. Her language, reflected in MacSweeney's crystal clear translation, is grounded and tranquil, at times contrasting with the turmoil of grief and isolation that Barrera feels throughout her travels."
    —*ENTROPY*

"Through a genre-bending mix of memoir and literary history, *On Lighthouses* exhaustively explores the lighthouse's contradictory figuration as an emblem of escapism, which nonetheless remains firmly rooted in relation to a specific geographic place."
    —*PUBLIC BOOKS*

ON
LIGHTHOUSES

ON
LIGHTHOUSES

Jazmina Barrera

Translated from Spanish
by Christina MacSweeney

TWO LINES
PRESS

Originally published as *Cuaderno de faros*
© 2017 by Jazmina Barrera
c/o Indent Literary Agency
www.indentagency.com

Translation © 2020 by Christina MacSweeney

Two Lines Press
582 Market Street, Suite 700, San Francisco, CA 94104
www.twolinespress.com

ISBN: 978-1-949641-34-9
Ebook ISBN: 978-1-949641-02-8

Cover design by Gabriele Wilson
Cover photo by Simon Jones / Millennium Images, UK
Typeset by Jessica Sevey
Printed in the United States of America

Library of Congress Cataloging-in-Publication Data:

Names: Barrera, Jazmina, author. | MacSweeney, Christina, translator.
Title: On Lighthouses / Jazmina Barrera; translated from Spanish
by Christina MacSweeney. Other titles: Cuaderno de faros. English
Description: San Francisco: Two Lines Press, 2020. | Includes bibliographi-
cal references. | Summary: "Includes general explanations about lighthouses,
literary references, legends, and personal experiences." -- Provided by
publisher. Identifiers: LCCN 2019034279 (print) | LCCN 2019034280
(ebook) | ISBN 9781949641011 (hardcover) | ISBN 9781949641028
(ebook). Subjects: LCSH: Lighthouses--United States--History. | Barrera,
Jazmina--Meditations. Classification: LCC VK1023 .B3713 2020 (print) |
LCC VK1023 (ebook) | DDC 387.1/550973--dc23. LC record available at
https://lccn.loc.gov/2019034279. LC ebook record available at
https://lccn.loc gov/2019034280

3 5 7 9 10 8 6 4 2

This project is supported in part by an award from the
National Endowment for the Arts.

For Lucía and Marina,
whose names are light and water

CONTENTS

44° 40' 36.4" N 124° 4' 45.9" W
Yaquina Head Lighthouse. Brick tower painted white, 28 meters high. Original Fresnel lens, visible at 31 kilometers. Blink pattern: two seconds on, two seconds off, two seconds on, fourteen seconds off.

Yaquina Head

We arrive in Portland, Oregon, to stay with Willey, my aunt's boyfriend. In his youth Willey had been an EMT and a member of the Black Panthers; he had a daily routine that included a full breakfast of ham, eggs, wheat semolina, and toast, reading the newspaper, and smoking two or three cigarettes on the balcony of his home.

I don't smoke, but during my first day in that house I spent a long time on the balcony watching the river with its boats and seabirds. I guess that's equivalent to smoking. The following day we took the highway south. My cousin—two meters tall—and I were squashed in the back seat of the red pickup Willey referred to as "my baby." We spent a night at the snow-capped hotel where *The Shining* was filmed, en route to the crater of an extinct volcano that is now a sapphire-blue lake.

Two years later, when I returned to Portland with my mother and aunt, Willey drove us to the coastal city of Newport. It was September. In that same pickup, we traveled along a wooded highway, stopping at a diner halfway to our destination to eat cupcakes made from locally grown marionberries, served by a couple of kindly old men. I remember that I had my headphones on, and was looking out the window at the forests of bare trees with trunks that were first dark, then white, and finally red. In Newport, I felt I'd never before seen an ocean so gray, so cold. Even in summer, the whole city is shrouded in mist, and you have to search for your hotel among the clouds.

*

The great majority of my collections have been failures. When I was small, I used to admire those children who had all the Knights of the Zodiac figures, or the series of collectable toys that came in bags of potato chips. I tried my very best, but never achieved that form of prowess. Two collections that became quite extensive though were my gemstones (I now know they were all varieties of quartz) and my marbles. I was fascinated by the colors and texture of those glass spheres, which is possibly the reason for my choice. My collection of dried flowers also prospered: I still have it, specimens from the gardens that have been part of my life.

My largest collection is of books. As a child I used to read them the day they were bought. Up until adolescence, every book I owned had been read. Then came the moment when I had more books than time to peruse them, and I soon realized that I'd probably never read everything on my shelves (there is a Japanese word for it: *tsundoku*). I'm now able to divide that collection into two categories: the books themselves, as objects, and the reading experiences, which can also be coveted and amassed.

*

Even before I ever saw a lighthouse, I dreamed of one; it was abandoned, far from the coast. At the foot of the building was a garden and the house where I lived with my parents. In my childhood dream, I asked my father what he'd found during his exploration of the crumbling rooms. "Just the skeleton of a bat," he said. I insistently asked for reassurance that the animal was dead, but he only muttered to himself, like someone in the trailer for a horror movie: "Dead, but alive." The tip of the tower was visible: a dark garret where the bony hands of the bat's skeleton stirred a cauldron containing a potion. The camera then zoomed in on the skull, which in a squeaky voice said, "I'm brewing my revenge on the person who killed me."

✶

In *Moby Dick*, Melville says that human beings "share a natural attraction to water." At one point Ishmael offers an explanation for why people fritter away their savings and bonuses to visit such places as that sapphire-blue lake in the crater of a volcano, or a waterfall so high that the liquid evaporates before reaching the rocks, or a series of pools in the middle of the desert that are home to tiny prehistoric beings, or a natural well deep in the jungle. He explains the amazement we feel at the sight of the color now called International Klein Blue, or the turquoise of the Bacalar lagoon in Quintana Roo. Ishmael suggests that all men's roads lead to water, and the reason why no one can resist its attraction is also why "Narcissus, who because he could not grasp the tormenting, mild image he saw in the fountain, plunged into it and was drowned. […] It is the image of the ungraspable phantom of life; and this is the key to it all."

That reflective power of water made Joseph Brodsky believe that if the "Spirit of God" moved upon its surface, the water would surely reproduce it. God, for Brodsky, is time; water is, therefore, the image of time, and a wave crashing on the shoreline at midnight is a piece of time emerging from the water. If this is true, observing the surface of the ocean from an airplane is equivalent to witnessing the restless face of time.

No civilization bordering the sea, with lakes, or with important rivers has been immune to the need to navigate those waters, to explore the furthest reaches of the oceans, to transport or be carried on the waves. And yet mariners appear as vulnerable aboard their ships as penguins do ashore. Although familiar and necessary, water is also unknowable and menacing. Despite the fact that it makes up the greater part of the human body, it can also take human life.

The earliest lighthouses are the product of a collective effort to signal dangerous areas or the proximity of coastlines and ports. Shipwrecks may be less common nowadays, but for a long time they were everyday occurrences: 832 in English waters in the year 1853, according to Jean Delumeau; the author quotes Rabelais's character Pantagruel confessing to his fear of the sea and his terror of "death by shipwreck." And citing Homer, Pantagruel adds, "it is a grievous, abhorrent and unnatural thing to perish at sea."

The Hells of many mythologies can only be reached by boat, they are surrounded by water because, as Delumeau notes, in antiquity the ocean was associated in the collective mind with the most awful images of pain and death, the night, the abyss.

The Maya used to build monuments lit from within to signal places where it was possible or perilous to bring a boat ashore. The Celts used beacons to send messages along the coast. But it was the Greeks who gave these lights the name *Pharos*.

Fire indicating the sea's end. In *The Iliad*, Homer speaks of burning towers with bonfires that had to be constantly fed, like the sacred flames in temples dedicated to Apollo. He compares the lustrous glow rising to the heavens from Achilles's shield to the "blazing fire from a lonely upland farm seen by sailors whom a storm drives over the plentiful deep far from their friends."

Apparently during the Trojan Wars there was a lighthouse at the entrance to the Hellespont, and another in the Bosphorus strait. Suetonius says there was once a lighthouse on the island of Capri, and Pliny the Elder mentions others in Ostia and Ravenna (he also warns of the danger of mistaking them for stars). Herodian refers to towers in ports "which by the light of their fires bring to safety ships in distress at night." These are the precursors of the lighthouse whose name passed into so many Romance languages: *faro* in Spanish and Italian; *phare* in French; *farol* in Portuguese; *far* in Romanian. Precursors of the "Pharos" of Alexandria. On the island of Pharos, visited by Odysseus, which "has a good harbor from which vessels can get out into open sea," there was a huge guardian lighthouse that Ptolemy I, the Macedonian general of Alexander the Great, ordered to be constructed in the third century BC.

It was a tower of some 135 meters, constructed from pale stone, with a glass dome crowned with flames and a statue of the god Helios. It's said that its architect, Sostratus of Cnidus, chiseled his name in the stone, plastered over it, and then inscribed that of Ptolemy on top, knowing that the plaster would eventually crumble so it would be his name that survived. The flame was tended day and night, and ships' crews could see it fifty-six kilometers offshore. It remained in existence longer than the Hanging Gardens, longer than almost any other of the seven wonders, until, in 1323, an earthquake brought it down. But Alexandria will always be the city of the lighthouse, a huge ghost set down in history.

"The same streets and squares will burn in my imagination as the Pharos burns in history," says the narrator of *Justine*, the first book of Lawrence Durrell's *Alexandria Quartet*. In this work, the protagonist merges with the city, both of them seductresses, tempestuous and unattainable.

Later, lighthouses began to spring up in other parts of the world. In Rome and the surrounding lands high towers, such as the one dedicated to Hercules in La Coruña, were located at the entrances to ports in imitation of Alexandria. It's said that, in his madness, the emperor Caligula declared war on Neptune and attempted to insult him by collecting shells on the seashore, but as Neptune made no response, the emperor decided that he'd won. He celebrated this victory "by the erection of a tall tower, not unlike the one at Pharos, in which the fires were kept going all night as a guide to ships."

Firewood was the first fuel source for lighthouses, followed by coal, and later pitch. Then came oil and gas lanterns, and with the availability of electric power, light bulbs were used in conjunction with the magnifying properties of Fresnel lenses: fantastic vitreous heads like prehistoric monsters that can transmit light for many kilometers.

The oldest lighthouses still in existence date from the Middle Ages. The Germans at times used beacons to warn sailors of the proximity of the coast. In those days the custodians of lighthouses were monks, who took on the task out of the kindness of their hearts. Their voluntary work was in contrast to the attitude of certain monarchs, who awarded themselves the rights to everything that washed up on their shores (men and women included). That is the reason for the prosperity of such lands as Normandy, where the swirling tides often swept ships onto the rocks. During this period giant pagodas that served as lighthouses were also being built in China.

In 1128, the Lanterna was constructed in Genoa; in 1449, one of its lighthouse keepers was Antonio Colombo who, according to several sources, was the uncle of the infamous seafarer Christopher Columbus.

*

Sylvia Beach Hotel in Newport was opened on a whim by two women with an obsession for literature. It's an enormous house full of cats and retired ladies who travel in groups and wear hats (close relatives of men who construct ships in bottles, of those who go on bird-watching vacations, and of those—of us—who collect tiny replicas of lighthouses). The hotel has a library in the attic and around forty rooms dedicated to well-known writers: there's an Emily Dickinson, a Walt Whitman, a Jane Austen, plus a Shakespeare, a Melville, and a Gertrude Stein (although the premises take their name from Joyce's patron, there is no bedroom dedicated to the author of *Ulysses*). The decor of the suites reflects the respective periods and tastes of the writers, with their complete works on the bookshelves. I would have loved to sleep in Virginia Woolf, with its Victorian furnishings and a window looking out to sea, giving a distant glimpse of Yaquina Head and, on its promontory, the lighthouse. I'd just started reading *To the Lighthouse*: it's not clear to me now if it was a matter of chance or, knowing that I was going to visit such a building, I forced the coincidence.

The lighthouse in Woolf's novel takes its inspiration from one located on the coast of Cornwall, where the author used to spend the summer with her family: a small white structure with many windows, built on an island. *To the Lighthouse* opens by a window, with Mrs. Ramsay's promise to her son James that the following day, if the weather is good, they will visit the lighthouse near their summer home. Later, she repeats this promise while knitting a pair of socks for the tubercular son of the lighthouse keeper. Mrs. Ramsay imagines the keeper there, alone, week after week during the stormy season, the waves breaking against the lighthouse, rocking its foundations, covering it in surf. Directing her words to her daughters, Mrs. Ramsay says one should take lighthouse keepers "whatever comforts one can" because it must be terrible and very boring to be shut up there for months on end with nothing to do.

∗

I live on an island, on the fifth floor of a red building. The plaque in the hallway says it's the fifth, but for reasons no one has been able to explain to me, there are two second floors. I rarely leave this brick tower. When I do, it's almost always at night, or to visit lighthouses.

There are four windows. Two have bars that were installed a while ago when a burglar managed to get into the neighboring apartment. The other windows look out onto a brick wall a meter away. That wall is so high that, looking up, you can't see the sky. And neither can you see the ground below: the gap narrows and the bricks are lost in darkness. I've never suffered from claustrophobia, but I sometimes feel an uncontainable need to see the horizon. In this city of tall buildings, that horizon is difficult to find; in order to see anything at any distance you have to go up to a roof, to the river, or to one of the streets that cut across the whole island. From time to time I do one of those things. When I was taking art classes, I learned that my mind often follows the lead of my eyes, and if I restrict my gaze for too long, my thoughts become myopic.

Another problem with the apartment is the darkness. In my bedroom and in the living room a gray, muted, cloudy-day light filters through the windows. The only plant I've had here died after only a few weeks. I spend the whole day bathed in artificial light, and to see the sun—if the sky outside is clear and there's no one else home—I have to press myself up against the bars of the other window and search it out above the buildings.

I wonder what will become of me, spending so much time without direct sunlight; I wonder if I'll turn into one of those blind, transparent fish that live in subterranean rivers and caves.

It feels as if my nerves are a little more sensitive than the norm. I faint at the prick of a needle; almost all strong emotions give me a headache. Perhaps it's that I'm not thick-skinned, and people seem a permanent source of danger.

Pain has this ability to become stronger when you think about it. If I concentrate hard on a part of my body, it ends up hurting. If I concentrate hard on myself, I hurt. For instance, right now, as I write this. By contrast, when I visit lighthouses, when I read or write about lighthouses, I leave myself behind. Some people like gazing into wells. That gives me vertigo. But with lighthouses, I stop thinking about myself. I move through space to remote places. I also move through time, toward a past that I'm aware I idealize, when solitude was easier. And in moving back in time I distance myself from the tastes of my own age, when lighthouses are linked with unfashionable adjectives like *romantic* and *sublime*. It's difficult to talk about the topics generally associated with lighthouses: solitude, madness. Those of us who try have no option but to accept ourselves as quaint.

If I focus my attention on myself, the pain is magnified. On the other hand, when I think of myself in relation to a lighthouse, I feel brand new and so tiny that I almost vanish. What I feel for lighthouses is the complete opposite of passion, or at least it's a passion for anesthesia. Analgesic addiction. I'd like to become a lighthouse: cold, unfeeling, solid, indifferent. When I see them, I sometimes have the sense that I really could turn to stone, and enjoy the absolute peace of rock.

I understand the objections to the desire to escape from the world. I know it can be an egoistic, arrogant desire, the attitude of someone looking down from above, from a tower. That's why I find lighthouses so attractive: they combine that disdain, that misanthropy, with the task of guiding, helping, rescuing others.

✷

Robert Louis Stevenson says that to tour light-houses is "to visit past centuries," which is exactly what he does in his book *Records of a Family of Engineers*. With the help of letters and diaries, he unearths the stories of his father, Thomas, his grandfather, Robert, and the latter's stepfather, Thomas Smith: all engineers and inventors, pi-oneers in the creation of lighthouses.

The Scottish coast is a place of rough seas, stormy skies, bleak headlands, "savage islands and desolate moors." The year was 1786, and along the whole coastline, only a single point shone out: the Isle of May, with a tower dating from 1635 on top of which was a grate with a coal fire. In 1791 the beacon was the cause of a conflagra-tion in which the custodian of the lighthouse and five of his children died. The sole survivor was a girl who was found three days later, permanently transformed by the sight of the flames reflected in the sea.

The Isle of May was the only light on that coastline of shipwrecks and pirates: a single, in-adequate light. For this reason, that same year the authorities decided to construct four more lighthouses. This task required engineers—not yet known by that name—whose responsibility it was to build the towers, light the fires, and, starting from nothing, create, organize, and recruit the members of a new profession: the lighthouse keeper. Stevenson's grandfather and Thomas Smith teamed up with the Board of Northern Lights to illuminate certain strategic points on the coast.

The engineer as artist. Stevenson describes his father's and grandfather's profession as if he were talking about Romantic poets. The engineer, as a Wordsworth or a Coleridge, makes his plans with an eye to the natural world. His task does not involve language, but nature itself. For this he needs the ingenuity (the word engineer is derived from Medieval Latin *ingeniator*, meaning someone who creates or uses an engine) and intuition, which Stevenson calls a "sentiment of physical laws and of the scale of nature." His "feelings" have to capture the smallest detail. To calculate the height of waves, for instance, the engineer had to take into account the slope of the ground, the configuration of the coastline, the depth of the water near the shore, and the species of plants and shellfish on the site. His observations and instinct stood in for the instruments that would come later with the Industrial Revolution. Stevenson recounts that he often watched his grandfather for hours on end, counting the waves, noting when they receded and when they broke. His task was to predict the unpredictable: how the new structure would affect the tides, increase the strength of the waves, hold back rainwater, or attract lightning. And all this done in the open air while sailing angry, inhospitable seas or, back on land, with only a tent to sleep in.

Villagers also constituted a threat. Superstitious, accustomed to war and violence coming from the sea (the Vikings had arrived in ships), they believed a man saved from the waters would be the ruin of his rescuer. On one occasion, Thomas Smith was mistaken for a Pict (the Scottish tribe that spoke Pictish) and if it hadn't been for Robert Stevenson coming to his aid, he might have been summarily hanged. Years later, Robert himself was suspected of being a spy: when he happened to ask about the state of the lighthouse in one village, they almost put him to death.

In 1814, Sir Walter Scott traveled to Scotland with Robert Louis Stevenson's grandfather aboard the lightship *Pharos*, accompanying a team of lighthouse inspectors. During the voyage Scott wrote a diary in which he mentions Bessie Millie, an old woman who lived in Stromness and earned a living selling favorable winds to seamen. No one ventured to set sail without first visiting Bessie Millie, who prayed for the winds to follow the sailors on their voyage. In order to reach her house, which Scott described as "the abode of Eolus himself," he had to walk along a series of dangerous, steep, rocky paths. Bessie was close to ninety, skinny and wizened as a mummy, and had a kerchief that matched the pallor of her cadaveric body tied around her head. Her blue eyes shone with the gleam of madness. "A nose and chin that almost met together, and a ghastly expression of cunning" gave the impression that she was Hecate, the Greek goddess of the night and ghosts, says Scott.

The family of Stevenson's grandfather was replete with pious women and moribund children, but neither poverty nor illness quenched his thirst for knowledge. In the winter months, when voyages were impossible, he sought shelter at the University of Edinburgh. He studied math, chemistry, natural history, agriculture, moral philosophy, and logic within the stone walls that housed Charles Darwin and David Hume during those same years.

He was the first person to construct a lighthouse on a marine rock, far from the coast. Bell Rock had been the cause of many shipwrecks, and it was said to be haunted by the ghost of a pirate. Years later, Robert Louis Stevenson's father also contributed to the development of lighthouses when he transformed the Fresnel lens by combining it with metal to increase its strength.

"Perhaps it is by inheritance of blood," says Robert Louis about Cape Wrath, "but I know few things more inspiriting than this location of a lighthouse in a designated space of heather and air, through which the sea-birds are still flying."

*

Impossible to imagine a lighthouse without including the sea. They are a single entity, but also opposites.

The sea stretches out to the horizon; the lighthouse points to the sky.

The sea is in constant motion; the lighthouse is a static watchtower.

The sea is changeful, a "battlefield of emotions," as Virginia Woolf might put it. The lighthouse is a stoic, immovable man.

The sea attracts by its distant sound, beyond the dunes. The rays of the lighthouse call out through mist and high tides.

The sea is a primeval liquid; the lighthouse is solidity incarnate.

The sea, the sea, is a biological, mythological metonym for the feminine. The lighthouse is masculine, phallic.

The sea is the empire of nature. The lighthouse is the artifice that, in its dignified smallness, opposes nature.

*

Willey took us to a restaurant with a sea view and we ordered fish and chips. In the late afternoon we visited the dock, where dozens of seals were vying for space on the wooden planks, tumbling on top of each other and quarreling with very human sounds. The pilings of the dock were covered in starfish that looked like warty hands, and there were seagulls perched on the mastheads. In the distance, to the west, the sun was disappearing behind mist-shrouded forests. Out to sea were rocks spilling over with seals and beyond them, hidden by cloud, the lighthouse.

When the sun had set we returned to the hotel and I browsed the literary souvenir shop (mugs in the form of Shakespeare's head, postcards of Don Quixote, Charles Dickens plush toys). Later, my mother and I walked down to the beach, where mist merged the water and sky. Pure gray. Two blurred figures were embracing on the sand. At some point we found ourselves engulfed in mist, startled, with no idea in which direction the hotel lay. We walked blindly as darkness fell. Then, in the distance, we made out a blinking light.

In a scene from *To the Lighthouse*, as the sun goes down, Mrs. Ramsay reads James a story about a storm at sea. She hugs him, wishing that her children would not grow up so quickly. She will never again be as happy as in that moment,

JAZMINA BARRERA

she thinks, while they are still young. As she comes to the end of the story, she sees something in James's eyes, "something wondering, pale, like the reflection of a light, which at once made him gaze and marvel." Mrs. Ramsay turns to look over the waves and sees "two quick strokes." The lighthouse had been lit.

*

Some time after that trip to Oregon, I attempted to articulate my feelings about that panorama—the moment and the lighthouse. While I was writing, I realized that there was something more, something in the lighthouse itself that intrigued me. It wasn't just the fact that both the characters in the story and I were moving toward something; that something had to be a lighthouse. I started to research the history of lighthouses, the stories surrounding them. And it was like falling in love; I wanted to know the lighthouse to its very core. All lighthouses. Everything about lighthouses.

I'm aware that this hobby isn't original; it's almost as common as collecting porcelain

29

figurines or postage stamps. We're attracted by the image of the lighthouse and that is, in fact, all we can retain of them: their form and image. Collecting lighthouses *per se* is utopic. What's more, the majority of lighthouses are government property, so it's impossible for them to pass into private hands. There is no sense in building a lighthouse for personal use, although you can live in one. Even so, the lighthouse would be a vessel; it would take possession of its inhabitant rather than the inhabitant possessing it. There is a perverse aspect to ownership, in that the possessor of an object has the ability to isolate it from the world, shield it, hide it away for personal use. But it isn't possible to completely possess a lighthouse because its function is to guide others, direct them; if its light goes out or is eclipsed, it will no longer be a lighthouse. It will be reduced to a shell.

That is the paradox of collections: they distract attention from the use inherent in the object onto the object itself; the same is true of poetry—where the emphasis is on language as a system and not its function of transmitting an idea—and of ready-mades, where an object taken out of context ceases to be a urinal and becomes something else. Except that a lighthouse can't be removed from its context. Or at least not completely: the medieval English managed to transform many Roman lighthouses into the towers of their churches and castles. Yet the moment they were distanced from the sea, they stopped being lighthouses.

When Robert Stevenson constructed the world's first lighthouse situated on a marine rock, he used the rock itself as the foundation. The lighthouse is anchored to the shoreline, to the sea and to stone, it is what it is and where it is.

*

The word *binnacle*, formerly *bittacle* from the French *bitacle*, meaning a small dwelling, refers to a sort of cabinet affixed to the deck of a boat, near the helm, which acts as a housing for the compass. In Spanish, *bitácora* has also come to refer to the logbook in which mariners noted daily events, and which is protected from storms and other disasters within the binnacle. Just as with the black box of an airplane, the logbook could be consulted to determine responsibility for the vicissitudes of a voyage, and to prevent future errors.

Like its marine equivalent, the lighthouse logbook is organized chronologically, and the keeper uses it to record technical and climatological information, any mechanical faults and the ways in which they are repaired. Its main function is to note the lighting-up time, as proof that this did in fact occur.

Robert Stevenson kept a travel diary, although it was more a list of occurrences than a compendium of stories and opinions. It did, however, contain a great deal more personal information than would be found in a lighthouse keeper's log. This diary was written on ruled paper and had an index, as if he foresaw his grandson consulting it, or was conscious of the pioneering nature of his task and wished to preserve the details of the story. There is a great deal in that diary that is "useful and curious," wrote his grandson, much that is "merely otiose;" and much that is "an attempt to impart that which cannot be imparted in words." Robert Stevenson used to spend hours talking about his work, explaining to his son how to measure, how to know, to foresee, when in fact he was guided by instinct more than instruments. While these lengthy explanations bored his son, Stevenson found in his grandfather's diary "the whole biography of an enthusiastic engineer."

Otiosity, boredom: the logbook of a sailor, of an engineer, of a lighthouse keeper is a monotonous list of observations and figures. It would seem as if all the days were the same, give or take a storm. As repetitive as the movements of the lighthouse's beam. In the words of the Spanish writer Menchu Gutiérrez, "the unvaried rhythm of the light, its flashes and moments of darkness, placates memory and dissolves like ink in the well of the mind." Anesthesia in the memory of lighthouse days. When time is indefinite, the calendar and the clock become indispensable to avoiding paralysis. And for that reason the logbook is a constant point of reference, the only means of combatting boredom: each day less, one more X on the page. For want of an interlocutor, it is possible to construct narrative time in a diary.

✶

That night in Newport I slept in the only available room: Edgar Allan Poe. On the desk was a stuffed raven, an axe hung from the ceiling over the bed. I felt at once ridiculous and excited reading "The Raven" in the dim light, lying under the red velvet comforter, facing the portrait of a young girl. I didn't then know that the view from the window was also part of the Poe memorabilia. I hadn't read his last text, an unfinished story about a lighthouse keeper. The next day we begged to be moved to any other room because Edgar Allan Poe really was quite disturbing. We were given Hemingway, which, although less gloomy, had a plethora of guns and stuffed cats.

We didn't get to the lighthouse the following day either. Willey had already mapped out our whole itinerary, and drip-fed us information about what was going to happen next. We had breakfast in a restaurant overlooking the sea, with the lighthouse as a constant presence. Then we visited the aquarium, where I recall getting as close as I could to a pair of otters, until I bumped into a sign informing me that the females were in heat and might be aggressive. The aquarium also contained a wide variety of fish and mollusks, but for me the most thrilling experience was the area called Sandy Shores, where the sea anemones lived.

When I was ten, I visited the Montreal Biodome, which is a sort of zoofari divided into ecosystems. My favorite was the tropical rainforest because it had a tank containing rocks covered in wonderfully colorful freshwater anemones. When touched, they would suck your finger with their pink or orange tentacles. It was like interacting with a bed of flowers: anemones are the most vegetal animals in the world.

In *To the Lighthouse*, Nancy touches the soft anemones "stuck like lumps of jelly to the side of the rock." She then imagines that the pool is a gigantic submarine world, full of whales and sharks, and she is changed into the God who causes misfortune and desolation when its hand blocks out the sun falling on the water. Later, Nancy raises her eyes to the trees and the sea, and what she views there seems so vast, and the world in the rock pool so tiny, that it is suddenly as if "her own body, her own life, and the lives of all the people in the world" were reduced to nothing.

*

A couple of years ago I went to an exhibition of James Turrell's light sculptures at the New York Guggenheim. The second piece was a column of white light, a line shining on an equally white wall. All the visitors gravitated toward it. Light, according to Turrell, occupies space, it has mass and is sensed through sight, but also through touch. Anne Carson says light is neither observed nor breathed, it is just a pressure that is felt. She describes it as "being in the same room as a man you love." Both the artist and the writer agree on a sense of pressure, of interaction with the body. John Berger also says that light is ubiquitous and felt, it "places a hand on your back. You don't turn round because from a long, long time ago, you recognize its touch."

Humans absorb light through their skin, they eat light. But even so, they persist in trapping it. Light can be found at the root of our lust for gold, our fascination with cinema and photography. In the same way, ships are attracted to lighthouses, like insects toward a lamp. Because a lamp, a lantern, a flare, a candle, a match are all small lighthouses whose light also demands, summons, convenes.

*

Two, four, six, eight, nine. The sun goes into hiding in Ireland. Two, four, six, eight, nine. In Howth, the Bailey Lighthouse shines through the night. Its beam has the rhythm of two, four, six, eight, nine so that ships don't confuse it with a distant house, thinks Leopold Bloom in Joyce's *Ulysses*, as he lies stretched out on the sand. It's the twilight hour and Gerty is coming onto the strand with her siblings. Bloom watches her as the sunlight dwindles, and other lights make their appearance: fireworks, church lamps, and the lighthouse. The stars have come out, but there is still enough light to observe Gerty's shapely young legs.

People are afraid of the dark, thinks Bloom, and light is a kind of reassurance. Light won't harm them. Gerty realizes that Bloom is watching her and understands that he wants her. Then a shadow stirs. Black, as Bloom knows, is the color that absorbs most light. Gerty sees the bat and uses its presence to allow Bloom to look under her skirt at her legs, and higher.

The bat is a friar, a little man, thinks Bloom. With its tiny hands, always flying, who knows why. He thinks it must live in the belfry because the species likes shadows and solitary places. It occurs to me that the bat would also like to live in the top room of a lighthouse. I can imagine it sleeping there, after dawn, hanging from the ceiling, darkness hugging itself.

*

I'd like to be able to write this fragment in the present tense, as a tribute to the few lighthouse keepers who remain, but it already feels like an imaginary present.

At one time almost all lighthouses were tended by keepers, working in shifts from six in the evening to midnight, then midnight to six in the morning. Stevenson recounts that in his grandfather's day there were as many as three men in the tower, but they sometimes coincided so infrequently it was as if they were alone. But cohabitation could also be wearisome. That changed after one of the keepers in the Eddystone lighthouse died, and the survivor was obliged to live with the corpse for days. According to Stevenson, the keepers often spent their time bickering, which to his mind was not necessarily a drawback because, in that way, they kept watch on each other, making sure each fulfilled their duties. Living with others in a lighthouse was so difficult—reports a Scottish documentary film—that in England, until recently, the main requirement for becoming a keeper, apart from passing exams in geography and navigation, was an ability to get along well with people.

Depending on the location, every month, quarter, or year a replacement would arrive, an event the lighthouse keepers always spoke of warmly. The weeks ashore were compensation for their hard work. They could see their families, sleep well, move around as they pleased. Since lighthouses tend to be located at dangerous points, when they were on an island, landing and setting out to sea again could be problematic. In the past, when communication with the outside world was impossible, there was always the fear that the relief keeper wouldn't appear. That something would happen to him on the way, no one would realize, and the lighthouse keeper would be left without means of survival.

*

The hours go by in Newport. The pages turn in *To the Lighthouse*. The years pass, and James finally makes his way to the lighthouse aboard a boat. As a boy, his father had never allowed him to go; the weather was always too bad. But now his wish will be fulfilled. He doesn't go to the lighthouse as ships do, seeking the coastline, but to the lighthouse itself. To the lighthouse converted into the archetype of a promise, the expectation of happiness that can sometimes be confused with, or perhaps is, happiness. Another of Virginia Woolf's characters feels that happiness lies in its anticipation, in the hope of happiness. One summer day, while dressing to meet her beloved friend Sally Seton, Clarissa Dalloway employs Shakespeare's words to express her joy: "If it were now to die 'twere now to be most happy." The past is beautiful, says Woolf, because "one never realizes an emotion at the time."

✳

There are experiences that are lived in a historical present for as long as their memory is evoked, with the full knowledge that the memory will be revisited in the future. It was a twenty-minute drive to the Yaquina Head Light, followed by a ten-minute walk from the parking lot. Formerly known as the Cape Foulweather Lighthouse, it is a twenty-eight-meter white tower with a black tip.

The lighthouse comes slowly into view between hills covered by a patchwork of yellow and white flowers, and those grasses that move in the wind, which Virginia Woolf might say are always on the point of fleeing "into some moon country, uninhabited of men." It grows, closes in, and shows first its tip, then the lens with its copper belly, followed by the observation platform, the tower, and the door to the house beneath. Woolf describes her lighthouse as "distant, austere." And she goes on to write, "So much depends…upon distance." From afar, a lighthouse is a ghost, or rather a myth, a symbol. At close quarters it is a beautiful building. Once you're inside, it ceases to be that, because a lighthouse is direction and never a point of arrival. Even when I was inside, I continued moving, up the iron spiral staircase leading to the tip, where the Fresnel lens, whose light is visible at a distance of thirty-one kilometers, was located.

The Pharos, the *faro*, the *phare*, the *farol*, the *far*: the house that is not only home to and protector of the light, but also transforms it into language. Its light speaks. Gives warning of points of danger, sandbanks, reefs; it signals a nearby port; tells how far away it is and identifies itself by its blink pattern. The Yaquina Head Light flashes two seconds on, two seconds off, two seconds on, fourteen seconds off. The lighthouse that Mrs. Ramsay sees in Woolf's novel has two short flashes followed by a single long one.

We spent only a few minutes inside the lighthouse. Once back in the open air, we were stopped by a sign saying, "Look for Whales!" And scarcely a minute had gone by before we saw two (or were there three or four?) humpbacks. Gray on gray: the whales, the waves. I've read that no one knows for certain why they leap from the water, and I'd like that to always remain the case.

We then went down to a small beach replete with perfectly smooth black pebbles and strings of green seaweed. There are two photographs of me sitting on a large rock on that beach. My face isn't visible; I'm looking out toward a horizon outside the frame of the photo. I wonder, now, what was there. Clouds? Ships? I seem to recall some black birds hopping nearby on the rocks.

What I definitely remember is turning to look at the lighthouse and having the sensation that it was very distant. As if it had never been there. Because even when you reach the observation deck lookout over the vast ocean to the horizon, there by the light source itself, you never reach the lighthouse. And neither did James, who was disillusioned to find that the one he finally visited didn't match his childhood imagining. Experience sometimes falls short of memory, and sometimes it's memory that can't achieve the heights of experience. The memory of this trip, my words telling what I recall, will fall short of what it was. The preposition in the title to Woolf's novel contains the whole of story, always approaching the lighthouse, which is above all an ideal, memory, promise: the inaccessible. What moves us.

*

I collect lighthouse maps. I have one that shows all the coastal lighthouses in the world, and another, from France, with a drawing of each lighthouse with its distinguishing features. That map came in a book I bought in the Paris Musée National de la Marine. Not long ago, I moved and it was the only thing I took with me to decorate my new walls.

I also have a *Cuaderno de faros de México*, which lists all the coastal lighthouses in the country, with the characteristics of their lights, their color, reach, and location: "Faro Sur Isla Arena, 20°, 37'; 90°, 28'. White, cylindrical reinforced concrete tower, 10 meters high. 300mm lamp. Photovoltaic cells."

My way of trying to understand lighthouses has been to draw plans of their interiors, their guts, their staircases, their former and present lights. But I also speculate about other schemes; I imagine ways of representing both faces of the lighthouse in a single image, showing its whole surface as if unfolding a paper cylinder, or reproducing the rear of the building, its front, and its top all at the same time, like a cubist portrait, in order to contemplate the lighthouse in its totality.

*

Just before his death, Edgar Allan Poe was working on a story about a lighthouse keeper and his dog. The keeper had no name, but the dog did: Neptune. "Large as he is," says the lighthouse keeper, Neptune "is not to be taken into consideration as 'society.' Would to Heaven I had ever found in 'society' one half as much faith as in this poor dog: — in such case I and 'society' might never have parted." Neptune is the name of the Roman god of the seas, and the dog in Poe's story is a water dog, the keeper's only companion. He doesn't take the place of society, he exceeds it. He is unadulterated company. Pure company.

Basenji are central African canines, members of the pariah dog group, with two particular characteristics: they have no smell and don't bark. But they do emit a surprisingly different sound, more a song than a bark or howl. Half dog, half ghost. "Basenji is my African dog," says the first line of Menchu Gutiérrez's novel of the same name, about a lighthouse keeper and his dog. "Basenji is my African dog. A soulless dog, mute as cold stone."

And Basenji is also like a shadow, the shadow of the lighthouse keeper, following him so closely that the dog sometimes feels it is the keeper. Its presence is silence personified, made animal, made tangible.

Years ago I had a black Labrador named Night. She liked swimming in fountains. Rather than a canine, she was a marine mammal, like a sea lion. She never barked, but would make sudden sounds with her jaws clenched shut, not dissimilar from those of a seal. But those sounds were exceptions: the rest of the time she mooched around the garden like a deep shadow.

✳

All that can be heard inside a lighthouse is white noise. Perhaps a TV or radio. But before the radio, there would have been, at most, the sounds of birds, the wind, the throb of the machines, and the monotony of the sea. After spending sufficient time inside a lighthouse, who wouldn't begin to hear a song in the sounds of the machinery, a voice in the wind or the waves?

✳

I grew up in a house on the outskirts of the city, where noises were rare and distinct. I remember the dogs at night, a cock crowing at dawn, and the jingle of the ice cream truck. The next house I lived in was also very silent. All the windows were double paned and looked onto a quiet street. Now, in this apartment, I can hear so many things at once that I have a hard time identifying them. There's the noise the heating system makes all day long, like some old wild beast. Then there are the neighbors; for example, a woman with a very shrill voice and a

Chihuahua. I never know to whom she's speaking because I only ever hear her voice, the music she plays, and the Chihuahua barking when it smells me nearby.

Then there are the footsteps, at all hours. I know that they come from the hallway, but I hear them from the ceiling. At night, there's a noise I haven't yet worked out, a deep, heavy, distant noise. I've speculated that it comes from the subway.

And the pigeons. There are always two or three, but never the same two or three. They wake early, at around six in the morning, and perch on the cornices. They make a kind of clucking sound and I can hear their wings beating against the outside wall when they attempt to fly.

I've never been capable of reading when there is noise or music playing. I can't even do it in libraries, surrounded by silent multitudes.

Every night, I have to put in earplugs to prevent the noises of the city from keeping me awake. The earplugs don't completely block out these noises, but they do muffle them. Everything sounds distant, except for my breathing and circulation, which are very close. The effect is like the sea or what must be heard in the mother's womb.

I wonder how far I'd have to go to hear silence. Or at least some form of silence, because at sea there are always waves, in the countryside there are the sounds of the wind and animals. And wherever I am, there will be my respiration, my heart. When it occurs to me that there isn't a single place or moment in which you can hear (or rather not hear) absolute silence, I experience a sense of anguish. Perhaps silence can be found in anechoic chambers, which absorb sound waves, or in outer space, or in death.

40° 51' 1" N 73° 56' 49" W
Jeffrey's Hook. Conical iron tower, 12 meters high.
Red and white lantern post with 300 millimeter lens.
Single flash every three seconds.

Jeffrey's Hook

Certain landlocked cities have lighthouses. On such rivers as the Rhine, the Seine, and the Saint Lawrence, lighthouses gave warning of dangerous areas. In London, the Trinity Buoy Wharf light is still in existence. This hexagonal, pale brown brick structure is located in an area known as Container City. I remember my father telling me about these buildings when I was a child. To my ears, accustomed to the Spanish language, the word *container*, which I never completely understood, sounded warlike; I imagined gigantic metal constructions, improbably conical or spherical in shape. It never occurred to me that they would be like shoeboxes.

When I visited that shoebox city, the shipping containers, adapted to function as housing, reminded me of the futuristic cities of nineties movies and TV series. The lighthouse on the wharf looked out of place among the container architecture, yet, like all of its kind, it was experimental in origin. For a time the building was used to train lighthouse keepers, and later to trial the lanterns and lenses that would then be transferred to other lights. It was there that the scientist (and bookbinder) Michael Faraday worked on the fixtures for the South Foreland lighthouse in Kent. A tiny museum at the foot of the lighthouse offers a display of Faraday's instruments and personal effects.

Today the Trinity Buoy Wharf light has no lantern. It doesn't illume, but it can be heard because it now has a bell.

The lanterns of lighthouses are the bells of churches. As with light, sound waves can also announce and convene. And in this lighthouse there's a bell that chimes ceaselessly. A bell that will sound for a millennium. It's made up of many other bells that chime according to an algorithm designed by Jem Finer. Apparently one day, in almost a thousand years' time, the music of the bells will come into a harmonic alignment, in a process that can be likened to the planets moving into alignment in the heavens.

✳

On the Manhattan shore of the Hudson, there is also one remaining lighthouse: Jeffrey's Hook, better known as the Little Red Lighthouse.

The city seems to peter out. The blocks of buildings disappear at a highway crossed by a footbridge, from which the only view is cars, trees, and the river. At the far end of the footbridge is a park that I visited with Lorena when we were together in New York for two weeks: my first since moving there, her last before returning to Mexico City. We shared her apartment in Washington Heights during the apex of the summer heat. I can't remember how we first met. It's as if she was always there with her delicate hands and hair that is in fact chestnut, but in my mind is red. It was the dog days, a time for goodbyes, even the summer sun was saying its farewell to New York. We were walking along a winding path of tunnels and drawbridges over the rail tracks, with a view of the George Washington Bridge, which crosses from Manhattan to New Jersey. The gray of its soldered-metal engineering stood out against the undergrowth in the park. The path was descending toward the river. From the shoreline, beyond rocks jutting through the surface of the water between scraps of sunlight, the south tip of Manhattan was visible. Below the great bridge was a small red lighthouse. A lighthouse at the end of the island, at the end of the river, which Antonio Muñoz Molina calls "the lighthouse at the end of the Hudson."

I have no memory of how I knew of the existence of this building: I woke up one day recalling that there was a lighthouse under the George Washington Bridge, with no idea of who had told me, or if I'd read about it somewhere. I had to find it. Lorena hadn't originally planned to accompany me; she was leaving the following day for Mexico, and was glad to be returning home, leaving behind the hard loneliness that life in this city can be. But we were only one stop away. We wondered how there could be a lighthouse so close to the bustle and reggaetón of Washington Heights, so close to the subway, the banks, and the accountants. I was already feeling fond of the neighborhood, with its custom of filling the Sunday sidewalks with chairs, chat, and dominos; the *sopa de siete potencia* (misspelling intentional) and the twenty-four-hour fruit stands, where other substances were probably also for sale.

The Hudson here is not in fact a river, but an arm of the ocean. It has been a fishing ground since the times when the Weckquaesgeek tribe inhabited its shores, and there used to be ships that sailed from Albany to the city or on to the Atlantic. Shipwrecks were so common on this stretch of water that a red pole had to be erected to signal the danger. And red was also the color of the lighthouse, constructed in 1880; a small structure, today almost invisible beneath the bridge. Its size, color, and green tip give it the appearance of a toy.

At the last minute, Lorena decided to come with me. We'd expected to find an abandoned building, a lighthouse vanquished by the bridge and highway, a ridiculous anachronism. Instead, the smallest lighthouse in the world (or at least that is how it seemed to me then) retains enormous dignity despite being dwarfed by the bridge. It felt much more on our scale, belonging to our universe.

Around 1942, the author Hildegarde Swift watched the bridge being erected over Jeffrey's Hook, and wrote *The Little Red Lighthouse and the Great Gray Bridge*, an illustrated children's book whose main character is the lighthouse, saddened and oppressed by the construction. At the end of the story, readers discover that the bridge is its metal brother, and that the lighthouse gets to continue to fulfill its function of safeguarding boats.

When the authorities decided to sell the lighthouse, many of the children who had read *The Little Red Lighthouse and the Great Gray Bridge* protested. They started petitions and even offered to collect money to buy it, to the point where the auction was canceled. The property was transferred to the Parks Department in 1951 and the lighthouse fell into disuse. The lantern was not switched on again until 1979, when the building was placed on the National Register of Historic Places and restoration was undertaken. In 2002, the sixtieth anniversary of the publication of Hildegarde Swift's book was celebrated by, for pure nostalgia, presenting the lighthouse with a new lens so that it could continue to illuminate the night. It was saved, not for its utility or even historical value, but for the symbolic and literary meanings it embodied. People refused to allow life to be so prosaic, were determined that reality should imitate fiction.

Weeks afterward I returned to the lighthouse, this time without Lorena (missing her, envious that she was back home). It was the one day of the month when the building is opened to allow girls and boys to climb to the observation deck. There it stood, demonstrating to those children that it is still indispensable, and gets along splendidly with modernity.

*

Other metropolises that are far from the sea, and whose rivers have dried up or been channeled underground, have their own kinds of lighthouses. Mexico City's Torre Latinoamericana, for example, used to function as a lighthouse on the high seas for the citizens who had lost their way in the urban tides. In those days there was only one skyscraper on the labyrinthine streets of the city, a single tower from which Mexico City seemed to stretch out forever, like an ocean; just as from the Eiffel Tower, Paris can be viewed from one end to the other.

The Eiffel Tower is still the only lighthouse in Paris. No one would dare to move a stone of that city without first seeking authorization (authorization they should not be given). By contrast, buildings in Mexico City are demolished and others spring up by the minute, each one taller than the last. They compete among themselves as trees in the rainforest compete for sunlight. During my own lifetime the Hotel de México in the Colonia Nápoles succeeded the Torre Latinoamericana as the point of reference in the distance. Whenever I was lost, I only had to see it to be sure of which direction to take. But new skyscrapers appear every day now, taller than the Hotel de México, blocking my view.

In Manhattan there are so many skyscrapers that none functions as a lighthouse. The whole stretch of land is so densely populated with tall metal structures that, at street level, their summits are invisible. For the Manhattan pedestrian, the lighthouse is perhaps more down to earth: Central Park, that enormous oasis, the meeting

place from which one can set out in a new direction, is the point of orientation on the island.

The most beautiful pseudo-lighthouse I
know of in a city is the eleventh-century Carfax
Tower in the heart of Oxford. Its four faces are
all that remain of St. Martin's Church. On the
front of the building is a clock, with male figures announcing the quarter hours. The name
of the tower comes from the French *carrefour*,
meaning crossroads. It's said that for many years
the place offered shelter and a point of reference
to travelers, and it is still the building that every tour guide in the city recommends visiting.
Planning regulations forbid building higher than
the Carfax in that area of Oxford, and its summit
offers a view of the whole of the city, its sea of
spires and rooftops.

*

Lightships, or lightvessels, as they are sometimes
called, deserve a fragment of their own here. The
masts of certain Roman ships were hung with
iron baskets in which fires burned throughout
the night. Lightships were located in very deep

or dangerous waters, where it was impossible to erect a stone structure. They also acted as stand-ins for coastal lighthouses under repair, in which case they carried a huge sign saying *RELIEF*.

The greatest difficulty was in maintaining the stability of those vessels in tempestuous waters. It was Stevenson's grandfather who invented the most popular means of achieving this: the mushroom anchor. The vessel on which Sir Walter Scott and Robert Stevenson traveled, the *Pharos*, was the first lightship in England.

In the 1930s, the earliest automatic lightships came into service; decades later solar power began to be used to recharge their batteries. With no crew and no keepers, they were ghost ships. *Ignis fatui*, fatuous lights, like the will-o'-the-wisps said to sometimes float on lakes or over the sea. Phantom, fiery, foolish Pharos vessels.

*

The lighthouse is always different, depending on the time and the position from which it's viewed. There is the lighthouse in the distance, a diminutive life preserver. The lighthouse close at hand, where its size is imposing, revealing its origins as a temple, a tower, and a house of illumination. The lighthouse at different times of day: In the mornings, we see it surrounded by seagulls; at midday the sun dots it like an *i*, but in the evening, as the sun declines, they separate in a form of ritual farewell. At night, the lighthouse is a second, terrestrial moon. There is the lighthouse standing calmly beside the sea, and the lighthouse in a storm, a titan that resists and, in the words of Michelet, returns "fire with fire to the lightning bolts of the heavens." And, finally, there is the lighthouse swathed in mist.

*

The world is a cornucopia of objects for the lover of lighthouses: plastic and metal models, prints and postcards. In Mexico City, there are also bakeries and hardware stores called El Faro, and Faros is a brand of cigarettes (prisoners condemned to death had the right to smoke one before facing the firing squad, from which comes the expression *ya chupó faros*, which literally translates as "he's had his last drag of the lighthouse").

There are lantern stores in Chinatown and stands at *son et lumière* events that go by the name of Lighthouse, an interview show called *The Pharos of Alexandria*, lighthouse magnifying glasses, an art book entitled *Your Lighthouse*, a Christian sect in Los Angeles called The Lighthouse Church, and it's the main element of a John Maus album cover. Its image and form attract us the way its light attracts ships.

✳

Lying on the beach, Leopold Bloom remembers Grace Darling, the lady of the islands, the girl with her hair flying in the wind. In 1838, Grace was a young woman living with her parents in a lighthouse on the Farne Islands. One day a storm blew up, lasting longer than any other before it. Standing at the highest window with her spyglass, Grace spotted a ship, the *Forfarshire*, which the waves had thrown onto the rocks, splitting it in two. A number of survivors were huddled together, clinging to the wreckage, begging for help. The legend goes that Grace managed to convince her father that they must set out together to rescue the shipwrecked sailors. At the height of the storm, they rowed to the wreck and, while her father helped the survivors aboard, she kept the boat steady. They "tossed on the waves," says Wordsworth in a poem he wrote in honor of Grace Darling, "to bring Hope to the hopeless, to the dying, life."

Montauk Lighthouse
1910

Montauk Point, Long Island, New York.

41° 4' 15" N 71° 51' 25" W

Montauk Point Lighthouse. Octagonal sandstone tower, 37 meters high, painted white with a brown stripe halfway up. The beacon uses the VRB-25 optical system. Single blink every five seconds. Foghorn: two-second blast every fifteen seconds.

Montauk Point

Ximena and I have been friends for half our lives (we did the math not long ago). When we were in high school, we had many things in common: we liked the same music; we disliked the same people. Neither of us had a boyfriend. I believe we were in fact terrified by the idea, and clung to the childhood we both missed so deeply. We hardly ever went to parties, and when we did, never had too much to drink, as most teenagers did. One day, at a school dance we did attend, a male teacher told us that if we kept it up, we'd be forty before we reached our teens. Suddenly, we felt like a pair of elderly ladies in the bodies of teenagers: awkward and alone. But we were together, keeping each other company in that isolation.

Time passed, and although our lives changed a lot, we remained close. Ximena left the city several times—for France, Chiapas, Japan—but we kept in touch. I was able to tell her anything. Then she decided to go to Thailand to work as a volunteer with blind and orphaned children. While I was scared about moving to New York, less than five hours from Mexico City and with Mexicans everywhere, she was going to a distant continent, where she didn't speak the language and the culture was very different. I really admired her.

Communication was difficult. Her computer gave up the ghost. We wrote infrequently, but I did hear that, after finishing her voluntary work, she went on a silent meditation retreat. From there, she came to my apartment on one of the noisiest streets in New York. I'd thought that after such a long absence she'd have changed, but that wasn't the case. She had the same easy gait, the same (maybe a little less biting) humor, and the same love of walking for hours on end. We covered the whole of Manhattan on foot, talking about living away from home; we cooked and went to karaoke bars. It was just like before, like always.

The plan was to go to Montauk one Sunday in

October: four Mexicans (Ximena, Jorge, Elisa, and I) and Huáscar, a Puerto Rican friend. I wanted to visit the lighthouse; Jorge and Elisa adored *Eternal Sunshine of the Spotless Mind*, a movie in which the words "Meet me in Montauk" are central to the plot; Huáscar had offered to take photographs of the lighthouse; Ximena just wanted to come along with me. We'd spent weeks organizing the trip, but unforeseen circumstances complicated everything.

The problems began early on with a telephonic misunderstanding. That Sunday morning, I was supposed to pick up the laundry at 9 a.m. The woman who usually calls me to say when it's ready is Chinese, and has an accent I find very difficult to understand. So when I received a call from someone with what seemed like an identical accent, and didn't understand a word she said, besides "pick up nine o'clock," I assumed it was about the laundry, and said I couldn't drop by that day, and would come on Monday.

We arrived at the car rental office at nine to be greeted by a young Indian woman who said that earlier that morning I'd changed the reservation to Monday. As it was the long Columbus Day weekend, all the cars were taken so there was nothing to do but wait and see if they had a cancellation. We were already considering returning to our respective homes when the woman told us that there was in fact one vehicle available.

Halfway to our destination we hit a traffic jam. The GPS said there was only two hours to go, but the cars in front of us were either stationary or turning back toward the city whenever the opportunity arose. Jorge began to read. Ximena was silent. At each turnoff we optimistically thought the roadway would clear, but everyone was taking the same route as us. It was as though all of Manhattan were traveling to the lighthouse. That made sense: a long weekend, the sun shining brightly—perfect for a trip to the beach. The lighthouse closed at five; it was by then three in the afternoon. We were losing hope. We were also starving. Huáscar had been looking forward to fresh seafood, but it was not to be. We'd faint from hunger before reaching the shore. When we saw a diner called Princesa at the next intersection we decided to stop, already convinced we'd never make it to the lighthouse.

Jorge asked if we'd like to hear a lighthouse joke but, just as he was about to begin, the hamburgers and open-faced sandwiches arrived, so we all stopped talking and tucked in. Months later, he told me that joke: The captain of a ship stops by a lighthouse and asks it to move, because he has the king of Spain aboard. The lighthouse replies: You move, I'm the lighthouse.

When we'd finished our meal, we went to check the highway, and saw the same interminable line of vehicles. Resigned to our fate, we got back in the car. Huáscar invited us to imagine how frustrating it would be if the jam cleared a few meters farther on. No sooner said than done: after one more cross street, all the cars began to pull over, leaving the highway free. On the left, we saw a sign announcing "Pumpkin Picking" and a field with rows of the vegetable. I asked Huáscar what the fun was in picking pumpkins, and he told me there wasn't any. It literally consists of choosing one of the pumpkins in the field, picking it, and then buying it. People preferred a pumpkin covered in dirt to the lighthouse. If we'd been able to hold out for two more intersections, we'd have arrived at the light hours earlier.

By the time the pumpkin field was behind us it was very late, and as we weren't sure if we'd arrive in time, Huáscar put his foot on the gas. We passed a sign alerting us to deer on the road for the next mile and a half, and I wondered how the person responsible for erecting that sign knew. How was it possible to confine the deer to that mile and a half, to stop them going into nearby towns and entering houses? In the next town we saw two deer in the garden of a house with a pitched roof, grazing by the mailbox. When the highway returned again to the park, we saw the body of another deer on the road-side. Elisa said that some of the most kitsch endeavors of United States poets were their verses about roadkill.

*

Lighthouses were a throwback to the age of enlightenment. France was the first country to consider them as under the auspices of the government. Before that initiative, there's a story that when Louis XIV's corsairs kidnapped the keeper of an English lighthouse, the king requested that he be returned to his duties: "I am at war with England, not with humanity," he said. The French government encouraged the proliferation of lighthouses in the nineteenth century with the same humanitarian zeal that powered the French Revolution. For this reason, Michelet calls Gallic lighthouses "peaceful towers of most benevolent and beneficent hospitality."

A controlled flame is an indication of human presence: survivors of shipwrecks once used fire and smoke to alert possible rescuers. In Greek mythology, Prometheus conferred the language of fire and the knowledge of science on mankind. "The age of fire" is the name historians give to the stage in which the earliest traces of civilization—necessarily linked to fire and language—are found. Cooking, smelting, roasting, incineration all followed from it. Lighthouses speak in that primordial language of flame, and their message is, first and foremost, that human beings are here.

✳

We did eventually reach Montauk Point. The pine trees and houses gave way to a state park with low-growing vegetation. The red-and-white lighthouse appeared between the shrubs, with the keeper's residence at its foot. It was fifteen minutes before closing time, so we raced up the hill.

When George Washington visited Montauk in 1756, he was twenty-five, one year younger than Ximena and I. He was vacationing on Long Island and stopped at Montauk Point to tell his companions that he envisioned a lighthouse there, on the hilltop. On that coast of many mishaps, the survivors of shipwrecks were continually being washed ashore. Around 1789, soon after becoming president, Washington decreed that all maritime lights should be brought under government control. In the last year of his presidency the construction of the Montauk Point Lighthouse began on the very hill on which he'd imagined it years before.

We barely had time to visit the museum below the light, with its old Fresnel lenses and the original writing desk of the first keeper. The story goes that one Abigail, the wife of a ship's captain, survived a shipwreck only to die there in the lighthouse, and that her ghost still haunts the building.

While ascending the orange brick spiral staircase, we stood for a moment at two round windows to view the fishing boats surrounded by a flock of seabirds, attracted by the smell. The calm sea and initially blue sky gradually changed to a clear ultramarine, and then to a pensive violet. Inland, the sun was descending. We were allowed to stand on the observation deck for only a moment. I have no idea of the actual reason for this restriction, although the view was so beautiful that I found it easy to imagine people wishing to throw themselves from that high place.

In a poem Walt Whitman wrote from Montauk Point for the editor of the *Herald* he says that he stands "on some mighty eagle's beak," from which he observes "the tossing waves, the foam, the ships in the distance, / The wild unrest, the snowy, curling caps..." Despite the fact that we were able only to put our heads into the head of the lighthouse for a moment, like Whitman we saw "that inbound urge and urge of waves, seeking the shores forever."

We were soon back on the beach, surrounded by lumps of seaweed-covered rock that looked like wet dogs. In his novel *Montauk*, Max Frisch writes about a trip he made to that beach one weekend. He'd recently met a younger woman, Lynn, and they had decided to escape together for a few days. Frisch says that he wants to describe their time together without adding any inventions. He mentions several strolls along the same shoreline where we walked over the stones to the sand, littered with fish spines, tree trunks, and the remains of horseshoe crabs (prehistoric animals that have ten eyes, blue blood, and only come to land once a year, on a full moon). There was no one else on the beach. The only sounds were the waves, the wind, and the birds. The sea was by then a deep blue that, tinged by the late afternoon sunlight, appeared purple.

Frisch describes awkward moments, numerous games of ping-pong, the decision to part from Lynn after the trip and return to his wife. The lighthouse appears only at the beginning of the novel, and reappears at the end, when Frisch views it from the airplane taking him back to reality.

*

Huáscar was talking on his cellphone. Jorge and Elisa had eyes for no one else. I looked for Ximena, and saw that she had moved a ways off. I think she wanted to see the bay from the other side of a group of rocks. For the first time, she seemed different. When, some days before, I'd asked her if it had been very hard to spend ten days in silence at the retreat, she'd said no, it had been the easiest thing in the world. The difficulty had been speaking again; after that experience, almost all words seemed unnecessary, a waste of time. When I saw her from afar, I felt that a part of her had changed, that she would perhaps now always be at a distance from me. I sensed her to be more silent, more serene than before, and that pleased but also saddened me. We were still alone, just as before, but Ximena's aloneness was more luminous. In the retreat house, she said she'd realized that for a long time she'd been clinging to her pain. I was definitely still clinging to mine. I felt that Ximena had understood something I hadn't yet managed to grasp. Felt that she had a secret she would perhaps never be able to share with me.

When the lantern came on, its light was initially disappointing. Minimal. But then the sun disappeared completely, and I was afraid I wouldn't be able to find my way back to the car. I got to Ximena and took her arm. In high school, we'd always walked arm in arm, like old ladies. I have a collection of photos of elderly ladies walking that way. Just as we did in the darkness.

However faint its illumination, the lighthouse became indispensible, our only guide through the shrubs. Huáscar, on the other hand, preferred to use his phone as a flashlight.

*

In architectural terms, every lighthouse is unique, although certain basic elements are standard: the spiral staircase, a service room, the rail around the observation deck, and the dome or lantern containing the optical equipment. This equipment varies depending on the era; for example, in a mid-twentieth-century electrically operated lighthouse there would be a generator feeding energy to the two bulbs, and moving parts resting on a kind of railway track. The generator was activated by gear levers that switched on the light.

The lighthouse keeper's duties consisted of maintaining the equipment, the tower, the house, and the yard—if one existed—in good condition, and reporting any problems to the authorities. He would sometimes also have to check light buoys or markers (luminous floating signals marking a geographical zone or dangerous area). The most important task was the lighting-up ritual, which almost always took place an hour before sundown. To do this in an electric lighthouse, the switchgears were activated. For those operated by kerosene, the process was more risky: the keepers had to wear dark glasses to protect their eyes; then incandescent asbestos-fiber mantles were placed over the wick, a small lamp was lit and positioned above the apparatus, the gas compressor was opened, and with a rapid movement, the incandescent mantle lit. A great deal of care was needed when using the high-pressure vapor since it could cause fires. Whether the process was carried out using electricity or kerosene, the keeper had to note the lighting-up time in the logbook. He also had to calculate the amount of combustible material used, an operation involving the number of cylinders, pressure, and temperature (in Campeche, Mexico, for example, where the profession of lighthouse keeper still exists, these calculations are part of a bureaucratic ritual: the report on the consumption of materials, any unexpected events, requests for materials, acknowledgement of the receipt of combustible materials and spare parts, and acknowledgement of receipt of clothing and equipment must all be sent to the appropriate authority). After all that was done, it was then a matter of keeping watch, like the prehistoric women who guarded the flame in caves, like vestals—virgin high priests dedicated to tending the sacred flame of the goddess. For lighthouse keepers, the greatest crime of all was falling asleep. But sleep was forbidden at night in case the light went out or a ship in distress came into view; and during the hours when it might have been possible, the din of the machinery often kept them awake. As the lantern was generally switched off an hour after sunrise, lighthouse keeping was a nocturnal profession. Keepers, like bats, had to be able to see in the dark.

Île Vierge   Batz

Île Wrac'h   La Croix

Stiff   Île Louët (à louer)

Créach   Trézien   Cap Fréhel

Saint-Mathieu

La Miller

Sein

Penmarc'h/Eckmühl

Kerhir (à louer)

Les Poulains
Goulphar

Île d'Yeu

49° 43' 18" N 1° 57' 15" W

The La Hague or Goury Lighthouse. Unpainted granite tower with a cylindrical base, 51 meters high. 250-watts incandescent lantern, visible at 30 kilometers. Single white blink every five seconds. Foghorn: blast every thirty seconds.

The Goury Lighthouse

It's perhaps true that I like lighthouses because I'm disoriented. I always feel as if I'm adrift, which is why the image of the sailor lost on the high seas is so deeply disturbing. And then the lighthouse appears like José Gorostiza's "pale pastor of fishing boats," that lights the path of the sailor, the seafarer who has spent the night on watch on the prow, "his feet numb with cold," while the waves drive his boat onto the rocks.

The first person to suggest that this might be the reason for my interest in lighthouses was my aunt Chantal. She traveled from France to Mexico by ship as a young woman, after marrying Uncle Gabriel and almost winning a competition to find the person who knew the most about that destination, the prize for which was the fare (her photo and story appeared in *Le Monde*). In the end she paid her own way on a ship that docked in New York before heading to the Mexican coast. Since my childhood, she'd been blowing into our house like a tornado: she'd give me three kisses and a bear hug, a cigarette in her hand and a gift under her arm (usually books or candies). She wore floral prints, had studied at the Sorbonne, knew Latin, translated, was irrepressibly joyful, and had an unquenchable thirst for knowledge. Not even my uncle Gabriel's death has managed to diminish the spirit and impetus that at times prevent her from sleeping, and make her days, her life, work double time.

*

If a building has a personality, history, and memory, it's only reasonable that it has a name. Yet in most of the world houses are now anonymous: I'd love to know when and why that christening custom died out. However, in England and Venezuela, for example, many houses still have names rather than numbers, and there are old buildings in Mexico City that have their own monikers, written in capitals over their art deco doors: Martha, Elisa…sometimes in honor of the architect's wife. Such personalized dwellings are the exact opposite of those identical houses that spring up by the hundred in the suburbs of cities. There would be no point in naming those zombies.

Alternatively, what have always had names are ships. The Greeks christened their boats with the names of sea gods, in the hope that they would protect them on their voyages. The figureheads on prows represent the spirit of the vessel, and are often feminine. This explains why ships almost always have women's names, and why in English they are referred to as "she." The ship is the sailor's female companion in a world in which, for a long time, women were considered unlucky. There was also the superstition that a vessel with a masculine name was condemned to sink, as did in fact happen to a few: *The Titanic* or *The Poseidon*, for instance.

I prefer lighthouses with proper names. They are very rare since "the someplace lighthouse" is the general rule, as if they were inseparable from their geographical location. Lighthouses are on the frontier between civilization and nature: they are constructed on rock, of rock, next to water, between storms. Maybe they should follow the example of rivers and mountains, whose names seem to involve no human intervention.

Some have beautiful names, at times descriptive, like the Foulweather Lighthouse or Italy's Lanterna. There are others with names based on their geographical location that are also very evocative: Cabo Villano (Cape Villain) in Spain; Longships Light, off the southwest coast of England, bearing the name for Viking boats; Cape Disappointment in Washington State; Finisterre in Galicia (it was once believed that boats would fall off the end of the world there). In Sweden there is an island called Fårö, where Ingmar Bergman lived and filmed. It has fewer than six hundred inhabitants, who speak a dialect of Gutnish, the oldest language in that region. The word *Fårö* belongs to that dialect, and has nothing to do with lighthouses; its meaning is something like "distant island." The island has a lighthouse named Fårö Fyr (*fyr* does mean lighthouse). This white tower is one more character in many of Bergman's movies.

Many lighthouses have the names of people,

such as the Alfanzina in Portugal, the Kéréon in France, or the Charlotte-Genesee Lighthouse in Rochester, New York.

There are also those with nicknames more famous than their official titles, in the same way as animals and plants have common names more apt than their scientific nomenclature. This is the case of, for instance, the lighthouse on Fire Island, off the southern coast of Long Island, which is generally known as The Winking Woman due to its rapid blink pattern. Those lighthouses with feminine names are a counterpoise to the masculine image associated with the edifice, sailors, and lighthouse keepers.

*

It was summer when I met up with my mother and Chantal in the latter's apartment in Paris. That was not my first visit to the city, but seeing it again with Chantal was different. She knows the history of every church and street, and can transform those histories into anecdotes ("On that bench, I saw Marcello Mastroianni chatting with a *clochard* and offering him wine."). She prepared a banquet for us every night, and in the mornings showed us Paris. A few days after our arrival, we got the urge to visit another part of France, one that wasn't overrun with tourists.

There was a postcard with four views of Normandy on one of the doors in the Paris apartment. Each scene, showing a different season, had a repeated element: a man in a yellow waterproof jacket standing under an umbrella in the rain. With that image in mind, I packed a raincoat, an umbrella, and boots, and we boarded a train for Normandy. Upon our arrival, people were sheltering in the station, watching the downpour.

One of those people was Danielle, Chantal's nearly lifelong friend. Their parents had been close, and the two girls had grown up together. They were both in the habit of saying, perhaps as part of a philosophy of life, *c'est pas grave*. Danielle drove us to her home in a small car with a GPS and an alarm that went off every time she exceeded the speed limit. The farther we got from the station, the better the weather became. There were also fewer people and more cows.

We ended our journey in the town where Danielle lived with her husband, Jean Louis, a doctor. Jean Louis had white hair, a slow, deliberate way of speaking, and sad eyes that smiled when he welcomed us warmly in a Spanish we never dared to tell him was in fact Italian ("*Benvenutas!*"). He and Danielle immediately showed us our bedrooms and the bathroom; they had discretely placed a French/Spanish dictionary next to the toilet, just in case.

For dinner, Danielle had prepared a huge variety of entrées with cold cuts from who knows what part of the cow. Jean Louis asked us if we were not delighted with France, if we didn't think its history exemplary, its people adorable, its cows delicious. Any attempt at criticism was quickly neutralized by one of these rhetorical questions.

✳

Lighthouses are always assumed to have a gaze. They were called Polyphemus, after the one-eyed giant. One keeper called them "eyes of the night," as if they were part of that monster with a thousand eyes Chesterton said was the night. Another keeper commented that every window of the lighthouse was a different image, changing from day to day: "The view is there, looking at you," he recalled.

The sailor looks toward the lighthouse—his objective—but the lighthouse looks out to sea, or beyond the sea. Its eye is like that of the Greeks, sending out a beam of light to the end of the ocean, to the end of the world. The artist Tacita Dean made a video, *Disappearance at Sea*, in which she filmed from inside a lighthouse, using a mirror and a lantern to make the light reflect off the sea. The lighthouse looks and searches, as a human being looks, a human being of stone. The first time I stood before a lighthouse, I concurred with Michelet in feeling that "this guardian of the sea, this constant watchman" is a "living and intelligent *person*."

✳

Lighthouses also have voices. In terms of language, their light is voice (Philip Hoare compares the blink pattern of the lighthouse to a cetacean's clicks). And when the light fails, there is another voice: the horn. Fog is the worst enemy of the lighthouse because it's beam can do nothing against the milky density that swamps and diffuses it. At such times the horn is the hidden cry that calls out to ships. "The great deep cry of our Fog Horn shuddering through the rags of mist," says McDunn, the lighthouse keeper in Ray Bradbury's story "The Fog Horn." McDunn has seen prodigious sights. He has seen fish worship the lighthouse like a god; he has seen a gigantic prehistoric beast rise from the sea, called by the lighthouse's siren. It's believed that sailors invented sirens and their songs based on marine mammals: seals, whales, narwhals. The lighthouse has the same unfathomable, oceanic voice as those animals. If, as Lycophron the Obscure claims, the first lighthouse was in Partenopea, then it was named after the Greek siren Parthenope. According to McDunn, the siren, the foghorn, calls out like a "big lonely animal crying in the night. Sitting […] on the edge of ten million years calling out to the deeps." It is a voice "like an empty bed beside you all night long, and like an empty house when you open the door, and like the trees in autumn with no leaves."

On June 22, 2013, there was no fog over the North Sea. The sky was clouded, the waves gray, and over five hundred boats and a number of brass bands were gathered around the Souter Lighthouse to bid farewell to the foghorn. The voice of the lighthouse, like its light, became redundant after the advent of GPS technology. With this in mind, Orlando Gough composed his *Foghorn Requiem* to be played by the flotilla of boats, the brass bands, and the lighthouse siren. That day, the sound of the trumpets was part siren and part narwhal.

In Bradbury's tale, when the foghorn—the siren—sounds, a monster that speaks the same language as the lighthouse rises from the depths. It gazes lovingly at the lighthouse, moves closer, looms over it, and folds it in its strong embrace until the building is destroyed. The monster made the error of wanting to possess the lighthouse. It had learned, concluded McDunn, that "you can't love anything too much in this world."

*

The following day, after Jean Louis had made a reservation at a restaurant in Bayeux that served mussels, we set out to see William the Conqueror's tapestries. Jean Louis was at the wheel, and the whole journey was accompanied by the sounds of alarms: he never fastened his seatbelt and often exceeded the speed limit. *Danielle, mes lunettes!* he shouted suddenly, and stopped in the middle of the road to search for his glasses in every compartment of the vehicle, while the cars behind us honked their horns in desperation and Danielle prayed for patience, both in that moment and most likely in those that would follow, for all the lost spectacles of the coming years. The voice of the GPS giving directions added to the din. My mother, sitting in the back seat between Chantal and me, said it sounded like Nurse Ratched in *One Flew Over the Cuckoo's Nest*. At each traffic circle (French highways are littered with them), Jean Louis went around three times to ensure he took the correct exit.

When we'd seen the medieval tapestries (an enormous comic strip embroidered with betrayal, war, and shipwrecks) we went in search of Jean Louis's famous mussels. The rest of us had finished our entrées, main courses, and desserts before he'd managed to extract them from their shells and swallow them.

Cows were still the predominant element of the landscape, with the addition of granite houses with external beams, whose hydrangea-filled gardens lined the road with a flush of blue, purple, and pink until we arrived at our small hotel: a stone house with a sloping roof, surrounded by flowers and with a small stream. It was by then clear to me that the French can be temperamental, especially at 93 degrees on a summer's day. Those who don't go on vacation remain to work, without air conditioning, and we tourists are easy targets for their resentment. The hotel manager grudgingly escorted us to our room and, as we were entering, I commented that bees had gotten in (such an abundance of flowers has to have its downside). He killed the insects one by one, and I tried to help by closing the window through which another ten were about to fly, but with my characteristic ham-fistedness I managed to break the sash and was treated to a *mais, qu'est-ce que tu fais?* After the man had sorted out the window, I dared to point out that the keys didn't work. Would it be a problem to leave the door open? It depends on what you have in your luggage, he growled. I later understood that part of his ill temper was due to the fact that the bees had stung his hand. When he discovered that Jean Louis was a doctor, he asked his advice, and was told that a swig of calvados would cure him.

We got back into the car and drove along a narrow lane bordered by fields, houses, and cows, close to the shore and the blue—almost turquoise, almost Caribbean—sea. I was longing to walk on the beach, and couldn't see why Jean Louis would continue driving, repeatedly asking Danielle to phone all the restaurants in the area (it was Monday, so most of them were closed) to make a reservation for dinner. The weather was unusual for Normandy: brilliant sunshine and hardly a cloud in the sky. Our plan was to stay for just a couple of days, and this would probably be the only opportunity to contemplate the sea and that landscape without rain (that was precisely the case: the next day the rain and fog made it impossible to see your hand in front of your face). There were only a few hours of sunlight remaining and we were still in the car, heading for some restaurant or other. Then I saw the lighthouse in the distance.

Constructed from stone it was tall, very tall,

and was perched on rocks some kilometers off-shore. That was why Jean Louis hadn't stopped, why he'd driven on: he was going to the lighthouse. I'd allowed myself to be herded along like one more of the multitude of Normandy cows, and had not the slightest idea of the name of the place we'd come to, much less the name of that lighthouse. We parked at the quay and I walked over rocks pointing like arrows toward the lighthouse to get as close to it as possible. Chantal then told me that when she was a child her father used to buy her and her siblings special shoes for climbing over rocks on the beach in search of shells and animals. I'd have loved to be wearing those shoes at that moment; however, I scrambled along as best I could and investigated the small rock pools filled with green algae and yellow sea snails that crawled across my hand. Then I climbed higher to feel closer to the lighthouse. The lantern had not yet been lit.

*

There exist histories of lighthouse technology that are, inevitably, also histories of the relationship between humans and light. They begin with the discovery of fire and continue on to lanterns using coal, oil, or kerosene, move on to mechanically produced light (in that history would be Michael Faraday, a kind of Dr. Frankenstein in his lighthouse), and end with the digital technology that now produces light via automated systems located many kilometers inland. In the past, only Zeus might have been capable of thinking up all that is now being done with light: it is molded, given color, made warm or cold, suspended. Freezing light is the nearest humans have come to stopping time.

*

In his youth, Augustin-Jean Fresnel liked watching the light entering through the windows of his house in Normandy. Years later, in the second decade of the nineteenth century, he completed his grand project, with the aid of an optical engineer with a prophetic name, Soleil: the Fresnel lens brought about the greatest revolution in lighthouse history. The stepped surface allows for a large aperture and short focal length;

the lens occupies less space and uses fewer raw materials. It is, in addition, beautiful, like those monstrous animals that glow in the depths of the ocean. In 1825, after Fresnel's invention had been patented, fifty lighthouses were commissioned to illuminate the whole French coastline.

*

Perhaps because of its proximity to the forest of Chapultepec, I've seen a great variety of birds in my mother's garden. I remember a woodpecker, a falcon, several blackbirds, a pair of blackpoll warblers, and many, many sparrows. Always in motion, birds arouse the desire to capture, to hold them in one's hand and thus be able to observe them, if only for an instant. When I was young I was determined to photograph a hummingbird nest constructed in an ash tree. My grandfather had a Nikon that I'd learned how to use in order to achieve that aim. I took photos of the chicks even before they had plumage and were still being fed by their mother and father, and took more when the fledglings were beginning to fly, still close to the nest. But some area of the image was always blurred. At that time, I wanted to be a wildlife photographer and work for *National Geographic*; it was an ambition that lasted for a year, until someone gave me an underwater camera. With my new photographic equipment in hand, I made a trip to the coast, but all the photos were fogged, and the subsequent frustration put an end to my passion for photography. My interest in birds lived on, although it has never been as great as that of certain people I know.

I have an aunt and uncle who practice what they call "birdtrotting." They have traveled the world, visiting nature preserves and national parks to observe exotic birds, each armed with a very weighty avian guidebook and a pair of binoculars. Lourdes also has one of those wooden bird whistles, and Julio has a program on his iPad that can imitate the call of any known avian species. When they hear his ringtone, birds flock to him. Julio and Lourdes have designed bird friendly gardens in various Mexican towns. They filled each of them with fruit trees, ponds, and other lures, and nowadays they don't even have to leave their armchairs to see kingfishers, orioles, thrushes, flycatchers, and mountain bluebirds. Whenever they spot a new species, they look it up in their guides, and put a checkmark beside the entry to indicate that the bird in question has been added to their personal collection. In the nineteenth century, or even before, in the times of John James Audubon, the famous ornithological painter, it would have been a more common practice to add a stuffed bird in a glass dome to the living room furnishings. Now a checkmark, and if possible a photo, is considered sufficient.

A number of decommissioned lighthouses have been converted into bird observatories, as is the case of the one on the Isle of May in Scotland.

Obsession is a form of mental collecting. These particular forms—for birds and lighthouses—involve an accumulation of images and experiences. But my aunt and uncle with their birds, and those of us who collect lighthouses, have all the traits Walter Benjamin finds in the great collectors: a fervent yet controlled passion, the consciousness of being the conserver of relics (they want to rescue birds from extinction, or at least preserve their memory, just as I'd like to rescue lighthouses from invisibility or keep some of their stories alive), and the desire to be guided by the objects themselves—or animals in the case of my aunt and uncle. Bruce Chatwin stopped collecting art because the pieces anchored him to one place and he wanted to travel, but he discovered that travel was another form of tyranny since "as you go along, you literally collect places." Benjamin would agree that this type of collecting is an attempt to satisfy the vain desire to possess with an immaterial, intangible form of possession, not unlike what one might feel toward a loved one. There is the same concern that absolute ownership of another—of the other— will never be possible, that there will always be an unsurpassable distance between oneself and one's desires.

*

Bowerbirds live in the forests of Australia and Papua New Guinea. *Amblyornis inornata* is the Latin name for one of the seventeen species; they are described as *inornata*, meaning "unadorned," since, with few exceptions, they do not have colorful plumage, being mostly either brown, dull yellow, or completely black. They are named bowerbirds because the males patiently build nests over a number of years. These ground-level hideouts look like thatched huts or arbors. But in addition to being brilliant architects, bower-birds have another human characteristic: they are collectors. For one thing, they collect melo-dies; they are capable of imitating the song of the kookaburra and many of their other neighbors. Yet, for the female of the species, neither con-structing the largest and most complex of bow-ers, nor being the best ventriloquist in the forest is enough to catch her attention.

The males sometimes use squashed berries to paint the walls of their houses, but usually they decorate the bower with things they collect and hoard. The selection of objects is often based on color. Just as any collector may aim to possess the whole oeuvre of a single artist, the books of a certain period, the postage stamps of a particular country (because when you collect it is necessary to specialize if you don't want to end up col-lecting the whole world), the bowerbird decides on a single color or combination of colors and forages anything it can find in those hues: orange and pink flowers, small green stones, iridescent insects, but also coal, deer droppings, clips, and pieces of plastic. Colors and textures are not confined to particular materials. Sometimes a splash of red flowers and a pile of green beads can co-exist in the carpeting of a bower, but they are always in groups; those collectors know that without plurals there is no collection. The birds are also capable of stealing a key piece, that one lacking thing, from their neighbors. The only judge of when the collection is complete is the female, who follows the polyphonic calls to the nest and makes a general inspection. At times, one further ritual is needed (naturally, collecting must be considered a ritual, a repetition that produces new meaning with each addition): the female is offered the choicest treasures, or the male selects elements of the collection as accessories for his dance. If, after all this paraphernalia, the female is satisfied, she gives the male her genetic approval.

Isn't collecting, then, a product of civilization? Was gathering not one of the earliest purely human activities? Is it possible to separate the concept of collecting from culture? Or did all this exist before, in the most ancient genes we share with birds? It would seem that those avian species even have a notion of ostentation, of collecting to attract and amaze others. What I don't know is if there are animals whose collecting is a solitary activity, an end in itself, a secret.

*

Lighthouses don't come in pairs. (That is not completely true: in London, for example, the experimental Trinity Buoy Wharf light had a brother on the riverbank.) They are twinned with the crow's nests of ships from which mariners scan the horizon, the towers in which witches were locked up, or the one where the Lady of Shalott awaited the arrival of King Arthur. In a tower of his chateau in Perógord, Montaigne had a library where he wrote his essays. It was his place "to be by himself, pay court to himself in private and hide away," just as Quevedo's Torre de Juan Abad was his place for speaking to the dead. And Hölderlin spent over thirty years in the highest room of a tower, where a kindly carpenter cared for him during his period of insanity. Princesses like Rapunzel, human equivalents of the ivory tower, took refuge in them—far from the world, elevated above it, untouchable, possibly bored out of their minds, always awaiting someone or something. It is the prospect awaiting the prisoner, awaiting the person in the White Tower at the center of the fortress known as the Tower of London, in which hundreds of men and women spent their final days.

I wonder if anything waits for me in this tower. If so, I have no idea what it might be. Perhaps what I truly hope for (and I no longer know if it is hope/desire or hope/believe) is that nothing happens.

*

Lighthouses hold out against the weather and the sea in the same way ships hold out against the waves. "The sea is so great, Lord, and my boat is so small" is the prayer of French sailors during a storm.

Exiled in his lighthouse, the keeper is something akin to the shipwrecked man. A voluntary Crusoe. Just as the escapist flees from a dark past, a failed romance, or ideology, or a person might seek refuge in physical solitude for what he carries within him, for the lighthouse keeper, exile is a choice. The protagonist of Poe's last story, "The Light-House," has a thirst for solitude: "that solitude, / which is not loneliness." Loneliness is an emotional state. Solitude is the condition of isolation; it can be enjoyed, can be a pleasure that is at times physical.

"Clear passion, my everyday solitude," Cernuda termed it in his "Soliloquio del farero" ("Soliloquy of the Lighthouse Keeper"). That solitude, he says, fills itself with only itself. He abandons it one day, and then finds it again in the sea, the sun, the rain, and darkness, in desire and in mankind. Solitary truths that embrace him as he watches them from the observation deck.

> I am a diamond in the night that rotates giving warning
> to men,
> For whom I live, even when I cannot see them;
> And so, far from them,
> Their names now forgotten, I love them in the crowds…

In novels such as Verne's *The Lighthouse at the End of the World*, the keeper confronts the unknown exterior: the untamed, the wild. In contemporary stories of lighthouse keepers, the monsters are, by contrast, interior. When confronting these chimeras—personal or of others— the character of the keeper can become a hero. Yet he is heroic from the outset, having left the world behind and risked his life on an altruistic mission ("For whom I live, even when I cannot see them"). This sometimes contrasts with his misanthropy, his need to isolate himself, and converts him into a monk who removes himself from the world in order to pray for it. His work, while solitary, is for others ("And so, far from them, / Their names now forgotten, I love them in the crowds…").

The character of the solitary lighthouse keeper is also to be found in romantic imagery. Because lighthouse keepers (male or female: from the nineteenth century, or even earlier, several wives of the keepers worked in the light, and there were a number of designated "keeperesses") were not always so alone. On some occasions— when the light was located on the coast rather than offshore—there were two or three keepers, or more figures in the surrounding environment, such as visitors, companion dogs, or the keeper's dependents. In the electric lighthouses of the late nineteenth century, whenever possible, families, even whole communities, congregated around the light.

*

I haven't been able to visit any lighthouses since winter set in. I always mean to, but the cold makes it even more difficult to get myself out of the apartment. I've never before experienced such a complete awareness of the weather: I check the temperature every day, and am constantly finding new manifestations of winter that I don't know how to classify. I've discovered that it's less cold when it snows; sunny days are windy, and there is something called the "wind-chill factor" that makes the chill even chillier. I can't imagine how that happens. I've also discovered sleet, a miserable cold fluid, much more bothersome than simple rain or snow. I know that the days following a snowstorm are the worst: the snow gets slushy, and muddy puddles form at the corners. I still can't estimate the depth of those puddles, and I move around the streets with less elegance than usual. I find more and more ways to avoid going out unless it's absolutely necessary.

✳

On October 31, 1823, the packet boat *Paris* sailing out from New York was shipwrecked off the Normandy coast, near La Hague. The tides in that area are treacherous, with infernal currents and that bad weather that seems to laugh in the face of the people of Normandy. After the tragic incident of the *Paris*, as a part of the Fresnel Plan, the Goury Lighthouse was constructed. The granite and metal structure was erected on the Gros du Raz reef. The engineer, Morice de la Rue, boasted that the task did not cost the life of a single worker, despite the daily perils involved in constructing on marine rock. Goury has had an electric light since 1970; the last of the keepers abandoned the lighthouse in 1989, when switching on and off began to be controlled from the mainland.

*

In Mexico there is currently a total of three hundred lighthouse keepers. One of these, from Puerto Escondido on the Pacific coast, was interviewed about his daily routine: he has to get up early to communicate with the authorities in Acapulco, to whom the keepers of the coasts of Mexico report on sea conditions and the morning's weather. Like fishermen, keepers learn to detect minute changes in the waves, and to diagnose storms. There are occasionally miracles or mirages that break the monotonous scanning of the horizon. The Alacranes (Scorpion) Reef is the farthest from the coast in the Gulf of Mexico: since British ships were often blown onto these rocks, Queen Victoria decided to present Mexico with a lighthouse. The island on which it was built is called Pérez, and Sostén Efraín, the keeper, claims to have seen in the vicinity a species of island they call *Desaparecida*, because the island is "visible when there's an ebb tide, but disappears again when the tide is high."

There isn't much to do in a lighthouse, says the keeper of Puerto Escondido, except the ones powered by kerosene, where you have to operate a lever every four hours. But those were other times and other lighthouses, and what concerns him now is idleness and low spirits. In order to survive these two conditions, he recommends having animals in the lighthouse, a radio, and plenty of reading material. His work has affected his health: he suffers from chronic depression due to the loneliness of the prison he is locked in day and night, whether it is on the mainland or an island. Lighthouse keepers often used to be dropped off on islands without even a boat so they wouldn't go fishing or set out on a pleasure trip, leaving the lantern unlit. Now, a prisoner of the sea, of sadness, the keeper of Puerto Escondido sleeps all day. "On these islands," he says, "loneliness is a problem. It turns you into a philosopher." He also notes that lighthouse keepers often go mad, as happened on Clipperton Island.

That island was known as Isla de la Pasión until an English pirate, John Clipperton, gave it his own name. Rights to the guano deposited on the island (in the Pacific Ocean, 1,100 kilometers from Mexico) by the huge number of seabirds that inhabit it were disputed by France, England, and the United States before it occurred to the Mexican government that, having been part of Nueva España, Clipperton had in fact always belonged to Mexicans. In that area of hurricanes and reefs, the Mexican president Porfirio Díaz ordered a lighthouse to be erected on a high rock, which served as the basis for almost the whole building: all that was needed was the lantern on the summit and the keeper's house at the foot. Díaz also sent Captain Ramón Arnaud, his wife, Alicia Rovira, and over a hundred people to work on the island. Their provisions came from San Francisco since the Americans had still not given up on the whole affair. Later, once the American residents left, the Mexican population requested aid from their government, but the Revolutionary forces—the conflict was then in its early stages—sunk the supply boat. During the armed conflict in Mexico everyone forgot about Clipperton, and the islanders received no help. Months passed, and in 1914 an American ship ran aground on the reef surrounding the island. When another vessel arrived to pick up the survivors, the crew offered to take the Mexicans to Acapulco, but Captain Arnaud refused the offer, still confident of receiving supplies from Mexico. People began to die of scurvy, a condition that causes hallucinations. One day, the captain imagined that he saw a ship and ordered his men to accompany him to seek assistance. They all drowned. By 1917, there were only eight women, seven children, and one male left alive on the island: Victoriano Álvarez was the lighthouse keeper, a mixed race man from Colima, to whom Arnaud had granted ownership of the most remote spot on the island. When he became aware of this singular status, Álvarez suffered delusions of grandeur and proclaimed himself the king of Clipperton. During his reign, he raped and killed four of the women. Although the exact events are unclear, the official version is that the women put up with the abuse until the day Álvarez decided to claim possession of Alicia Rovira. They then organized themselves and killed him with a hammer. There is some doubt as to whether Rovira had a child by the lighthouse keeper. On the very day Álvarez was killed in 1917, the cruiser *Yorktown* arrived to pick up the survivors.

Loneliness and power had the same maddening effect on Victoriano Álvarez's mind as scurvy and despair had on Captain Arnaud's. The infants whom Frederick II of Sicily decided to isolate from all human interaction to see if they would begin to speak a primeval language—originating in pre-Babelian times—died despite having food and clothing. The absence of communication is one of the greatest dangers for a gregarious species like Homo sapiens.

The Puerto Escondido lighthouse keeper went on to speak of the many keepers who became alcoholics or were addicted to watching television (an English keeper remembers that whenever the sea was crashing against his tower, as if it were pre-planned, he'd lose his TV signal just at the most exciting point in a show). There are also keepers who have developed an addiction to reading, Quijotes who come away speaking "very correctly, like learned men, like Señor Carlos Monsiváis." The English lighthouse keeper said, "We used to have a lot of time on our hands, and when we read a book, we really read it."

"Every lighthouse had a story—no, every

lighthouse *was* a story, and the flashes themselves were the stories going out over the waves," says Jeanette Winterson in *Lighthousekeeping*, which I was reading this morning, really reading.

✳

My family has a house in the old part of Acapulco, near the Quebrada. We often used to go to the cliffs in the late afternoon to watch the sunset. You can only see the sun sinking into the sea from that side of town because, from the bay, the mountains hide it. The Quebrada has an amphitheater constructed *ex profeso* for watching the sunset, the same one that Diego Rivera painted over and over again from his house on La Pinzona, the adjoining cove.

It is also the cliff from which divers throw themselves each evening in a ritual that seems, but in fact isn't, ancient. With the first signs of nightfall, the bats come out. They are part of the stage show. It was there that I saw them for the first time, gently stroking the water with their wings, and then departing to eat the fruits of the night.

✳

In a song by Arcade Fire, "The Well and the Lighthouse," a man falls into a well while trying to capture the light of the moon. Due to that chimeric endeavor, he is trapped in the well, with the sky above his head. But in the end the man in the well saves himself. He is resurrected and dwells in a lighthouse, still a captive, but this time confined not by physical but by ethical bars: he can't abandon his tower because, if he were to do so, ships would be wrecked.

If the lighthouse is a solid tower of light, its mirror image is the well: an inverted tower of liquid darkness. Its antithesis is the bat, because the beam of the lighthouse is uniform, directed, and gyratory, while the darkness of the bat is erratic, chaotic, and unpredictable. The former emits geometrical light, the latter represents organic obscurity.

✳

In the visitor's center, Jean Louis inquired where he could get a good view of the lighthouse.

The woman told him that the best spot was a couple of kilometers away on foot, along the Customs Officers' Path. This trail, which extends over 2,000 kilometers along the coast from Normandy to Brittany, hugging the shore, was the idea of one of Louis XIV's ministers, Jean-Baptiste Colbert, who wanted to create a system for ensuring that exports were taxed, and the smuggling of contraband goods from England prevented. On this path, now worn by the feet of the many who have walked it, the coastguard had small watch-houses where they could take shelter.

After reaching the lighthouse, we continued along the shoreline, gathering shells, and then along the Customs Officers' Path, from which one can glimpse the small bay with its fishing boats, houses looking out to sea, and attractive gardens where vegetables, mosses, ferns, and hydrangea bushes grow. In the long dusk of the northern summer, the evening light fell on a house on the hilltop. It was identical, I thought, to the one in a painting by Hopper: seen from below, white, with a red roof, the sunlight striking it full on. I later looked at reproductions of the

painting and discovered that there was a lighthouse next to the house, a lighthouse I'd forgotten. It was the Cape Elizabeth Light in Maine,
painted by Hopper in 1927. The artist was another lover of lighthouses; they appear again and
again in his works, and were magnificent objects
for the study of sunlight at different times of day,
from different angles.

*

Jacques Prévert sent his friend André Pozner a
collage with a letter describing the piece as the
transformation of the Goury Lighthouse into "a
gigantic hourglass dressed in a sorcerer's amaranth robe and with the head of a wild boar."
(Prévert ended the letter, "Because I love you, I
do not forget you.")

The day after going to the lighthouse we
stood under the Normandy clouds and rain before the granite stone bearing Prévert's name in
the town's small graveyard, next to the church.
Then we went to the house where he spent his
last years composing songs, writing poems, and
making collages, such as the one he describes in

his letter to Pozner, in which the lighthouse represents time, but also himself, Jacques Prévert, wild as the boar and always wearing an amaranth robe.

＊

In 2011 Jonathan Franzen published the essay "Farther Away" about a journey he made to an island in southern Chile named Más Afuera (it is now called Alejandro Selkirk, and at one time was also known as Isla de los Perros—Dog Island—but I like to refer to it as Farther Away) in order to scatter a portion of the ashes of his friend David Foster Wallace. The original aim of the journey had been to take his mind off a personal crisis by bird-watching.

Franzen travels the globe to observe birds. For him, they represent "the remnants of a world now largely overrun by human beings but still beautifully indifferent to us."

There's nothing left in the world to discover, says the voice of ennui. Everything is now on the internet: every island, every bird, every lighthouse, and every lost civilization. There is no reason to go any farther: if it exists it can be Googled. Everything has already been said, written, attempted. The world-weariness from which David Foster Wallace suffered, and which, in conjunction with severe depression, would lead him to commit suicide, appears to be one of the ills of our time. For Franzen, birds were an escape route. He still remembers the day when, while Wallace was taking a nap, he studied Ecuadorian birds for a future trip, and thought about the difference between his friend's "unmanageable misery" and his own "manageable discontents": Franzen found it possible to escape from himself "in the joy of birds," but this was not possible for Foster Wallace.

Collecting is a form of escapism. By giving our attention—our desire, our will—to something outside ourselves, to its beauty, its order, its classification and accumulation, we're distracted from lack and emptiness. The act of bringing objects together can be calming in its repetition, like a mantra. Faced with the fear of an uncertain future—collect. Collecting lighthouses, for instance, offers a sense of direction, however arbitrary that direction might be. It becomes, then, not only a mode of escape, but also of construction. Flight can be creative.

The lighthouse that, for David Foster Wallace, carried him "farther away" from his addictions and fears was fiction. That is, until he finished writing *Infinite Jest*, the story of a family of geniuses in a future world where the years carry the names of products and where, nevertheless, many things are still the same. Almost two thousand pages long, the novel is obsessive in its description, its explanations of chemistry, medicine, and math. It should be no surprise that once Foster Wallace had handed in the manuscript, he lost his sense of purpose. What would be his last novel, *The Pale King*, wasn't meeting his expectations. He was afraid that perfection had been granted him once and only once. It was as if he'd completed his most ambitious collection. The ultimate attainment of the desired object is unbearable: it annuls motivation, annihilates meaning.

One late afternoon on the island, Franzen understood the moment had come to scatter Foster Wallace's ashes. But to do so at that moment would involve missing the chance to spot the rayadito, a local bird he longed to add to his collection. He told himself it was "O.K." That it was "time to accept finitude and incompleteness and leave certain birds forever unseen." The ability to accept that was a virtue that had been denied Foster Wallace.

*

Some of the lighthouses I will never see:
1. Extinct lighthouses: Alexandria and all the ones I can only imagine, recreate.
2. The lighthouses I will never have time to visit. Because it requires a great deal of time to reach a lighthouse, and to take it in. Its size is proportional to the space it occupies in the memory, the hours and weeks and months needed to assimilate it.
3. The lighthouses that have never and will never exist. Almost all of these can be substituted by history or fiction. I can read the lighthouses that are impossible to visit: those that have been destroyed, are remote or fictitious. That aspect of the collection can, however, never be completed; at this very moment, somewhere, a book is being

written about lighthouses that I won't read because I'll be unaware of its existence, or have no
means of getting ahold of it, or don't speak the
language, or lack the time to read it. I repeat to
myself that this is nothing out of the ordinary.
That it has to be accepted. And while the effort
might seem wasted if it is, from the first, a failed
project, I've come to the conclusion that the same
can be said of almost anything worth doing.

*

In La Hague the gaps between houses by the
roadside widened. It was all arable land, cows
and, on one side—blending in with the stone of
the hillside—a fortress that, as Chantal explained,
was used by the Nazis during World War II to
keep watch on the horizon, since they didn't
know which direction the Allied troops would
come from. Nearby is the area of the Normandy
landings, a place of pilgrimage for the many
people for whom that war has a fascination or is
still a palpable entity.

Chantal's father, for example, had lived in
a chateau that was occupied by the German

navy. The family was forced to reside alongside the men, and even became friendly with one of them who was a good chess player. The sailors left, but their friend returned later, begging for help: he wanted civilian clothes so he could hide from the Allies. Chantal's father was not at home that day, and the other inhabitants of the chateau didn't recognize him and so refused that assistance. Chantal says her father often remembered the chess-playing mariner, and was very sorry to have been unable to help. He searched for him for a long time, but with no success.

We continued along the Customs Officers' Path, between trees and the cliff edge, and I suddenly realized that Jean Louis, despite being older than the rest of us, was far ahead. To my right was the lighthouse, immobile, present, and to my left, Jean Louis, heading off into the distance. The importance of distance, the importance of distance in motion, time in motion, Jean Louis's distancing from us (his aging), the permanence of the lighthouse (its much slower aging process), the ebb and flow of the waves.

I eventually sat on some rocks to watch the setting sun. At a later date, I'd recall the lighthouse

I saw at that moment as being identical to Millet's in the painting called *Bateau de pêche*. The canvas has a sailboat in the foreground, a calm but fast-flowing sea under a cloudy sky, and to the left, a lighthouse, which I like to believe is the Goury. The whole scene is lit by warm, slanting sunlight. Time seems to have stopped in La Hague, where Millet was raised among the cows and peasant farmers. His house and the one opposite it are still identical to those he portrayed in the nineteenth century: the stone, the hydrangea, the cows, the lighthouse are unchanged. The light of the setting sun he captured in *L'Angélus* still tinges the wheat and sky of the Normandy coastline the color of champagne.

Jean Louis continued marching on until he turned at a boulder and disappeared northward.

*

Edward Hopper said that the lighthouse is a solitary individual who stoically confronts the onrush of industrial society. The campaign to automate lighthouses was controversial in many countries. On the one hand, the profession of lighthouse keeping has been, in more than one sense, inhumane due to its isolation and the brutality of the work in terms of the time and physical strength required; and then there is the noise of the machinery and the constant threat of bad weather. In Mexico, the keepers' pay is also an extra expense for the state, and many people have argued that they should be made redundant.

However, detractors of automation claim that keepers can't be replaced by machines as they have frequently been responsible for seeking assistance for vessels in peril or offering refuge to the survivors of shipwrecks. The lighthouse keeper of Puerto Escondido tells of how he spotted an unexpected shape on the horizon one morning: it was a tuna boat that had run out of fuel. He informed the coastguard and, thanks to his help, the sailors were rescued. "One of these days, we'll be finding people who have died of hunger and cold washed up at the foot of our lighthouses," said François Jouas-Poutrel, a painter and lighthouse keeper; "there will be no one left to deal with the evils of these areas." Some keepers are confident that the changes are part of a natural process. Others say that although they understand them, they also dislike them. But many displaced lighthouse keepers are against automation. They think lighthouse keeping is wonderful work and want their jobs back. They speak "like a captain who is forced to abandon ship."

*

Almost all general histories of the lighthouse begin with Alexandria, or before—from the times of the beacons of the Celts—passing through the Tower of Hercules and the earliest medieval lighthouses in France, England, Italy, Spain, and China to the proliferation of lighthouses brought about by Fresnel in nineteenth-century France, and then the most modern ones of the twentieth century. In a few years, this history might include references to the last lighthouses, when GPS and computers have put an end to the need for them. I wonder if one day they will all be decommissioned, and if they will then return to being temples of fire dedicated to the sea, fetishes of the superstitious and seekers of esoteric knowledge, who will keep alive the legends of shipwrecks, lighthouse keepers, and the ghosts that surround them. Or if they will be (as seems their destiny) turned into hotels, museums, relics for the amusement of millionaires, retired folk, archaeologists, historians, and the curious. Divested of their function, they are collectible objects. They now also have that attractive quality of ruins and decay. For melancholics, they are all the more beautiful.

When will the last boat arrive safely to port thanks to the beams of a lighthouse? Who will be the last lighthouse keeper in the world? Or could it be that the relationship between humans and the sea is so primordial that there will always be someone to switch on—using a button or some other future technology—a light for ships in distress or fishermen? Or perhaps they will shine out as temples or memorials to the thousands of people who lie at the bottom of the sea.

40° 46' 22" N 73° 56' 24.6" W
Blackwell Lighthouse. Cylindrical, octagonal, un-painted gneiss rock tower, 15 meters tall. Inactive since 1940. Ornamented light.

Blackwell

For the first time, I decided to go to a lighthouse on my own—to the Blackwell Lighthouse on Roosevelt Island. I took the subway to Queens and then a bus across the bridge. The bus was only half full and the few passengers there were gradually got off until I was left sitting alone in the back. I always make the mistake of doing my research after the journey, when it's too late: I had no idea that, from the nineteenth century up to the present date, the island has accommodated prisons, hospitals, and a psychiatric facility. So when the bus dropped me at one end of the island and I found myself surrounded by elderly people in wheelchairs I didn't know what to think. One of these people, with a badly bruised arm, gave me a kindly smile. It was a fall day, the air was clear, the sun mild, and the wind icy. I walked along the shoreline until I came to the overgrown park on the northern tip, where there were a number of geese and seagulls, plus men and women in electric wheelchairs moving slowly along the paths or sitting in the sun. The river is choppy in this stretch: the swell rises suddenly and waves break on the rocks. Constructed in 1872, the Blackwell Lighthouse (I love the idea of a lighthouse as a dark well) is small and gray. It is made from blocks of gneiss, a rock similar to granite, quarried on the island itself. The architectural style is known as Gothic Revival: a classical octagonal column with a base, shaft, and capital; leaf decoration just below the observation platform, and an octagonal light whose roof is covered in guano. During the whole time I was there, a lighthouse gull was perched there, keeping watch.

In the sky, a plane seemed to merge with a flock of seabirds; on land, the lighthouse merged with the skyscrapers and smokestacks across the river.

Roosevelt is the island of the island, the stronghold of the excluded: lunatics, the sick, criminals, and lighthouse keepers. It's said that one of the inmates of the asylum built a fortress near his residence because he feared a British invasion. The legend goes that this man also constructed the lighthouse and had the following inscribed on a stone at its base:

THIS IS THE WORK
WAS DONE BY
JOHN McCARTHY
WHO BUILT THE LIGHT
HOUSE FROM THE BOTTOM TO THE
TOP ALL YE WHO DO PASS BY MAY
PRAY FOR HIS SOUL WHEN HE DIES

Roosevelt Island is a satellite, attracted by the centrifugal force that is Manhattan. The residents of the Lunatic Asylum, as it was called, shared the nocturnal terrain of madness with the lighthouse keepers. As a contrast to the physical barriers that kept those marginalized people in check, I imagined the lighthouse shining through the darkness, and for the first time it seemed to me a signal asking for help rather than offering it. Its rays had succeeded in escaping the island, something that would perhaps be only possible for those confined there on the day of their death.

I returned to the bus stop at the gates of the hospital. Another man in a wheelchair approached for a chat. He said that he'd never seen me on the island before, and hoped I would come back soon.

＊

I have the feeling that I'm nearly there. Since I came here I've been watching myself slowly transforming into a sealed tower. I move around in the calm of indistinguishable days. My routine is so precise, I feel so sane, that I must be losing my sanity.

The danger lies in feeling too comfortable, becoming accustomed to the unchanging repetition of the days, the minimal interaction with others. From here I can contemplate death as a calm ocean, imagine that I'm plunging into it without fear, even with pleasure.

＊

All scenarios associated with the lighthouse are liminal. But perhaps the most extreme situation was imagined by Jules Verne in *The Lighthouse at the End of the World*. This novel is set in Argentina, at the most remote point on the continent. It's the story of a keeper who is forced out of his lighthouse by pirates and is deeply concerned that more shipwrecks might occur before he can return to switch on the light, and that the crew coming to relieve him might never arrive. When Verne wrote the novel, he was close to death. *The Lighthouse at the End of the World* was one of his last works and was published posthumously.

I read Verne's novel long before discovering the fragments, also published posthumously, by Edgar Allan Poe. My thoughts now return to Poe's unfinished story. I search for clues, indications in the plot that might suggest what happens next. The narrator repeatedly stresses the pleasure of being alone in the lighthouse. A cutter had had difficulty in landing and has now departed. There's mention of a dog, Neptune, who is his companion, and of a chatty fellow he's grateful didn't, in the end, accompany him; it wasn't the first time *one* man had managed the light. He speaks of some peculiarity in the echo within the cylindrical walls of the lighthouse when he says the word "alone." Now he is immersed in silence. The lighthouse has a room below the waterline and he's worried that the structure might be unstable.

This is how I imagine the story might continue:

It's late at night and the keeper is tending the light. He has only an oil lamp, which casts a dim light on his small, improvised bedroom on the first floor. Outside a storm rages. He can sense its force each time a wave breaks against the lighthouse. Neptune, most likely sleeping at the foot of the bed, suddenly awakes. He's restless, turns this way and that. He seems to have heard something. The keeper is cold, feels the icy damp like a frost covering everything. Glancing at the floor, he sees a small pool of water forming on the stone. Is there perhaps a leak? The wind and rain sound like voices, but what they say is impossible to distinguish since the echo throws them back and forth. The pool begins to grow. Neptune howls. The echoes become louder, are definitely recognizable as voices now, although what they say is still incomprehensible. It might be the voice of a former lighthouse keeper. If he had died there, he must be still trapped: ghosts cling to the solidity they have lost, to the hard rocks used to construct the lighthouse, they will never cross a whole ocean to find their bodies and final rest. At his feet, the water has covered almost the whole floor, a centimeter of freezing cold brine, and Neptune is howling loudly. I imagine the startled keeper piling everything onto the bed. The voice sounds more clearly. He opens the door and goes up to where the provisions are stored. He'd already removed them from their wooden crates, but now he repacks them and piles up the crates. Will the voice of the former lighthouse keeper pronounce his revenge? If he'd died in a storm like this one, he's perhaps one of those spirits who don't yet understand their death and need to relive it in another person, need to observe it to comprehend it. The water continues to rise. The keeper suddenly remembers Neptune. He feels his way down in search of him, his hands trembling, but the dog is nowhere to be found and the room is now rapidly filling with water. He ascends the stairs again, goes to the light to see if Neptune is there. He isn't. The water is rising and the noise of the storm has entered the building. The voice is less clear. The keeper thinks of the crates of provisions. He won't be able to survive without them. He runs back down the stairs, but it's too late, water has already filled three quarters of the storeroom. There is no way to reach the crates. He returns to the lamp, and thinks that the voice of the former lighthouse keeper might have been warning him. The storm continues unabated outside. The roof must also be leaking, because water is beginning to drip down. The cold makes his flesh ache. It's as if the lighthouse didn't exist and the keeper is standing outside in the storm, with the tide rising. Perhaps there is no lighthouse. Perhaps the real ghost is the lighthouse.

*

The signal station was a complement to the lighthouse, and was often incorporated into it. From it communication could be established with ships through Morse code, semaphore, or foghorns. Yukio Mishima committed suicide on the day after he finished writing *The Decay of the Angel*. The novel is the last in the Sea of Fertility tetralogy and recounts the final stage in the life of Honda, a man obsessed with the reincarnations of a friend who died when they were both young. Honda meets Toru, a teenage boy of astonishing intelligence and beauty, and imagines that he is another of his friend's reincarnations. The orphaned Toru works in a signal station and spends his days observing ships. He has an amazing talent for recognizing them at a distance and for perceiving the changes of the weather on the sea. His only friend is a very ugly girl who is convinced that she's beautiful. He, on the other hand, sees himself very clearly. The pride of knowing he is both beautiful and brilliant causes him to shun the world and take refuge in contemplation of the sea. When Honda adopts him and takes him from the station, his coldness and derision of the world lead him along a path to imminent destruction.

When angels are about to die, we are told, they no longer have consciousness of themselves and cease to shine. Toru, self-aware at every moment, emits a sort of cold light. The novel also refers to death as something resplendent. Suicide is an honorable, beautiful, brilliant death. Toru is a narcissist and he is magnificent. Through his work, he helps the ships. But he doesn't do this from generosity or from love, an emotion he is incapable of feeling. It's just his job. As it's the job of a lighthouse. There is no intrinsic goodness in either a lighthouse or Toru. They are dazzling, cold, and beautiful. Toru attempts suicide, but fails. He is left blind, observing nothing. The last image in the novel is a blue, perfectly empty sky.

Mishima had been planning his death for some time. He'd carefully thought through all the details of seppuku, as if it were part of one of his novels. I like to think that, in his final moment of lucidity, he managed to see the blue sky, the emptiness that is surely different from the true emptiness of death.

Verne, Poe, Mishima. I'm not superstitious (although at three I begin to doubt coincidence), but when I finished *The Decay of the Angel* I decided that I have to stop writing about lighthouses. I'm falling in love with an idea of beauty that at moments seems too much like death. There are collections that will always be incomplete, and sometimes it's better not to continue them. I could always try a new one; if the main thing is the act of collecting rather than the collection itself (Is it? Isn't the theme important? I've always known that it's an impossible collection. The essence is the verb *collect*, not the noun *collection*.), I'll have to look for other obsessions. I must leave the lighthouse, come down from the tower, confront the bustle, irreverence, and noise of dry land. Leave the island. (Return? Where? To whom?) Lighthouses will always be there when needed. And that endless contemplation of the sea and nothingness is inevitable, so there is no need to hurry its arrival. The other is ephemeral. It must be appreciated while it lasts. One must muster the strength to explore the continent inland.

ESTADOS UNIDOS MEXICANOS
SECRETARIA DE COMUNICACIONES Y TRANSPORTES

SUBSECRETARIA DE OPERACION
DIRECCION GENERAL DE MARINA MERCANTE

CUADERNO DE FAROS

MEXICO 1988

43° 34' 27" N 6° 56' 47" W
The Tapia de Casariego Lighthouse: 1859. Catadi-optric lenses with a range of 18 nautical miles. Blink pattern of three flashes of white light every nineteen seconds.

The Tapia Lighthouse

I bought this notebook to write a travel diary. It has a silvery cover with a drawing of a space-ship and a caption saying *I WANT TO LEAVE*. On the trip, I take my diary and a book by Sir Walter Scott: *Northern Lights: Or, a Voyage in the Lighthouse Yacht to Nova Zembla and the Lord Knows Where in the Summer of 1814.* Scott wrote this diary during the voyage he made with grandfather Stevenson to visit the lighthouses that the latter had built in Scotland. They sailed from island to island aboard a lightship called *Pharos*.

I'm longing to inaugurate the notebook but realize that I don't know how to write a diary. It's something I've never done. I haven't got a personal style and I have no idea of the conventions.

149

I do know that it should be written in the present tense, perhaps to give a sense of immediacy; some people only give facts, others elaborate and offer reflections. Yet others (the ones who make me most uneasy) talk to the diary as if it were a person, a friend or confidante. I'd like this diary to be a prompt for my memory. I prefer diaries that use shorthand, that eschew pronouns and don't bother to conjugate verbs. The diary of someone who lacks the time to compose calmly but who doesn't want to forget. That's, I believe, how Scott's diary functions: only what he sees, what he experiences.

JUNE 24

The journey was very long. Four changes to reach Oviedo. Almost a whole day. Agustín met me at the railway station and gave me a tour of the nearby towns and villages. They remind me of Normandy. There are cows, stone houses, and hydrangea, and the sea is also Prussian blue. The main difference is the trees. Here, there are palms in almost all the gardens.

I'm staying in a sixteenth-century house. It has ten or more bedrooms, but there are only three of us living there: myself, a German painter who knows no Spanish and doesn't want to speak in English, and Pili, who looks after the house and does the cooking.

I read Scott. Lighthouses appear in the book from the very start. They first visit the Isle of May, where the lighthouse is due to be demolished. Scott suggests that the demolition should be only partial, leaving picturesque ruins. Then they go to the Bell Rock Lighthouse and, in the visitor's book, Scott writes a poem in which the lighthouse speaks from the "bosom of the deep." The poem is called "Pharos Loquitur."

This afternoon I went to the beach, accompanied by the dog belonging to the house. It was like an unattractive fox and barked indiscriminately at all the animals, including the birds and cows. A hawk flew above us and I was afraid it would carry off the dog.

After visiting the lighthouse on the Isle of May, Scott returns to the ship to write his "foolish journal." I went back to the Palacio (as the house is known locally) to write mine.

Despite Agustín's pleas that she economize on food, Pili prepares huge meals, heavy with meat, oil, cheese, and potatoes. Today she made *fabada*, a rich bean stew, and I told her that my grandmother's pressure cooker had once exploded while she was making that dish. Pili said that she was almost blinded when one of her pans exploded in her face. She can't read. Her eyes tire very quickly. The last book she tried to read was *Dracula*.

In the evening, while Scott and his friends sing and play backgammon or piquet, I visit the Tapia lighthouse: a squat tower, constructed in 1944 and painted green and white, standing beside a very large house. The islet is connected to the mainland by a bridge from which I look out on the sunset and a fishing boat. Agustín told me that a lighthouse keeper named Orlando lives there.

As the sun goes down, the seagulls look black against the sky and I mistake them for bats.

I saw the lighthouse at night. I saw Ursa Major. I saw a firefly lying on the ground, motionless.

JUNE 25

The character in Beckett's play *Krapp's Last Tape* makes a recording each year on his birthday. If a journal is written every day, Krapp's tapes are a sort of annual. On the last birthday of his life he decides to go back over the earlier tapes and finds a fragment that begins: "the belief I had been going on all my life, namely…" Impatient, Krapp fast-forwards the spool and comes to this part: "great granite rocks, the foam flying up in the light of the lighthouse, and the wind-gauge spinning like a propeller, clear to me at last that the dark I have always struggled to keep under is in reality my most…" And the revelation is left there, unfinished. When I reread the pages of this diary, I feel the same as Krapp on listening to the old tapes: not enough time has passed and now I'd like to erase or fast-forward it all. The problem with the diary, the journal, the problem with everything in this book is, in fact, that it's the record of someone who existed in the past, and that person can't be erased, however ashamed I am, however bored or depressed I become.

In the meantime, I read that Scott travels to a fishing village. The streets are full of "drunken riotous sailors, from the whale-vessels." He complains about the customs in that part of Scotland, says that anyone can raise a circle of stone wherever he wants and grow whatever he likes there. He drops in on Captain Nicolson, who is unhappy because all the trees he plants in his garden die. He also visits the ruins of a Pict castle and says that the Picts were small people who knew nothing of arches or stairways.

I went along the riverbank to the beach and walked barefoot among the rocks. Another woman was there, also barefoot. She smiled and warned me about the dangers of walking on the slippery rocks without shoes. And as if we had known each other for a long time, she told me that she'd left her shoes at C's house. I liked the sound of that.

I watched the sun go down by the Tapia lighthouse. In a café, I met Marilú and one of her brothers, the lighthouse keeper's children. They had grown up in the lighthouse, their lives dictated by the tides. When these were very high it was impossible to leave the island, sometimes for hours, sometimes for whole days.

Marilú told me how her father started out as the keeper on El Hierro, in the Canaries. The lighthouse was far from the mainland, on the windward side of the island. The only way to get to it was by mule. The exam that lighthouse keepers had to take wasn't easy; they studied a wide range of subjects, including math, signaling, and oceanography. Those who passed started their working lives at the most remote lights. Marilú would have loved to be a keeper, but she decided against the career as it would have involved spending years on some godforsaken island. And only then if she was actually appointed to a light; it was more likely that, while waiting for one of the keepers holding a lifetime position to die and thus free up his post, she'd have had to work in an office, and that was the last thing she wanted.

Marilú used to accompany her father on his travels and met many keepers who embodied the stereotype: solitary, unsociable, good with their hands, and great readers. Her brother, who grew up in the lighthouse and later became a sailor, was just like that: he scarcely spoke two words to me and quickly left the café.

But their father wasn't a typical keeper. Marilú said he was very sociable, talkative even, and always pleased to meet new people. He began lighthouse keeping with his brother—there were originally two positions on Tapia—and, when the time was right, he married and had eight children who lived with him in the tower.

Instead of following in her father's footsteps, Marilú set up a small *hostería* in the port of Tapia and called it El Faro.

I wanted to ask more questions because she wasn't the sort of person who offered information spontaneously. But just at that moment I began to feel uneasy, was unable to think of anything else to say, and Marilú departed.

The firefly was still there on the ground in front of the house, motionless but aglow.

June 26

I enjoy observing the interaction between Pili and the German painter. She insists on keeping up a stream of chatter in Spanish, and he doesn't

understand a word she says. Pili is very concerned that he doesn't seem to like her cooking.
She made him three hotdogs: she has a German
cousin who likes them.

The places where Scott travels are perilous. The *Pharos* was nearly trapped in a cavern
known as the Orkney-Man's Harbour. Scott says
that the people of those parts are superstitious
and hard of heart. He understands the reason for
this, knows that when people are constantly ex-
posed to danger they can grow numb. He recounts that they believe in what they call *trows*;
creatures somewhere between dwarves and fair-
ies that steal children, sometimes steal people's
very essences and change them into melancholy
phantoms. They can also steal your heart, "like
Lancashire witches."

Today, after going to the beach to look out
over the sea, with the Faro San Agustín in the
distance, I returned to the house to sleep and remembered something else Marilú told me, which
I forgot to write down here: in the years after the
war everyone wanted to be a lighthouse keeper.
It was a privilege because they had a roof over
their heads and a regular supply of food.

The firefly is still there on the ground, but its light is dimmer.

June 27

A horse and a donkey live in the garden of the Palacio. I stood watching them for a while today. The horse wouldn't let the donkey near the water. There's no grass in their corral, but I pulled some from another part of the garden. They didn't trust me enough to eat from my hand. The two animals were mistreated by their former owners and Pili had rescued them. She said that she'd also rescued a dog that the neighbors were trying to bury, despite the fact that it wasn't dead, and a cat that the women who used to live in the Palacio had abandoned. The cat was badly wounded and Pili adopted and nursed it. But some time later the women caught the cat and burned it alive.

Scott falls from his pony but is unharmed. He continues to travel around the villages of Zetland, gathering stories. For instance, someone tells him that a monster lives in a local lake, a sort of enormous fish like an upturned boat. It appeared one morning and no one dared go near it, and then it disappeared on a windy day.

Today I thought of a story by Juan José Arreola about a married couple that live in a lighthouse with another man. The woman begins an affair with the second man and it's exciting, until things become as routine and boring as ever because her husband appears to be blind to what is going on. The lovers love each other "disdainfully, wearily, like husband and wife."

What else could those two characters in Arreola's story have done? An affair was the best solution to boredom. Situations like that, and like the one I'm now in, isolated from everything, are perfect for romantic fiction.

The setting and moment would be ideal for a fling if the German painter were someone else. I often forget he's here; I hardly ever see him during the day because he sleeps the whole morning and then hides himself away to paint, with only his bottle of whiskey for company. We eat at the same table but don't speak. It's as if he isn't present.

As she can't communicate with him, Pili complains to me. She says he's very messy, drinks too much and, since he gets up late, she can never manage to clean his room.

I didn't go out tonight and so don't know if the firefly is still glowing.

JUNE 28

I missed my stop. I was supposed to get off the bus in Jarrio, but somehow thought it would take longer to get there. By the time I asked the driver to let me know when we'd arrived, it was already too late. I got off, saw a man smoking a cigar in front of a store, and asked him if he knew how to get to the San Agustín lighthouse. He directed me straight ahead along the highway. I'd hardly gone five meters before the same man pulled up beside me in his car and said that since it was Sunday and he had nothing better to do, plus was going in that direction anyway, he'd take me to the lighthouse. He worked for a company in a nearby town. His first remark was to ask why I wanted to go to the lighthouse; he didn't like the sea, had suffered an accident as a child and since then had had no inclination to get into "anything that big." He also hated sea-food. The man's name was Marino, but I didn't comment on the irony.

When we reached the lighthouse, Marino kept well away from the cliff's edge, standing beside a monument to those who had died at sea.

1931 Luciano García Suárez, 1945 José Manuel Méndez García, 1949 Eulogio García Rodríguez, 1950 Severino Méndez Méndez, 1950 Rafael Fernández García, 1951 Balbino Suárez Fernández, 1954 José García Vello, 1954 José Antonio Velasco Fernández, 1954 José Manuel Fernández González, 1956 Francisco Díaz López, 1959 Segundo Suárez Sánchez, 1960 Gaspar Cabrera García, 1963 Juan Izquierdo Suárez, 1976 José Mejía Fernández, 1976 Ángel Luis Fernández Cabrera, 1976 Antonio Rodríguez Peláez, 1977 Miguel Aquilino Seten Suárez, 1979 Camilio Fernando Suárez Méndez, 1985 Enrique González García, 1995 José Ramón Suárez Méndez.

People went on dying at sea in 1995. People go on dying at sea.

There's no Sergio in the list. If this was a diary, I should say here that while standing, reading the names on the monument, reading the names of the victims of shipwrecks, I remembered my friend Sergio, who drowned in the sea. And perhaps I should remark on how strange it is that, in my mind, he'll always be young, while I won't, and on how unfair that seems to me, but also beautiful. Or perhaps I should mention how, although I believe in hardly anything, I do think that there's something sacred about dying at sea.

The San Agustín lighthouse is in fact two lighthouses. One is tall and thin with black and white stripes, built in 1973, the other is a small stone structure, no more than two meters high, standing by a rusty bell that was rung as a form of farewell to passing ships.

A man with a walking stick, who was taking a breather with his white dog next to the small lighthouse, told me that I'd chosen a very bad day for my visit. The afternoon was misty; it was impossible to see the horizon. Not even the rocks down below were clearly visible from the clifftop.

I read that night how the *Pharos* weighs anchor in the bay of Quendal, where Stevenson wants to visit a Danish lighthouse called the Ward (according to Scott, this is the most common name for lighthouses), and a nearby plot of land earmarked for the construction of another light. The area is rocky, has steep cliffs, a great many ships have been wrecked there. Scott looks over a cliff covered in "beautiful short herbage." He says it's the perfect place to compose an "Elegy upon a Cormorant" or to write "madness of any kind in prose or poetry." But he prefers to sit tranquilly on the grass and then slide down the slope.

June 29

A realization: I'm writing about Scott in the present and about my journey in the past. I feel as if what happened to Scott so long ago is more present than what I'm experiencing. I feel that the written experiences of others are much, much closer than those I've lived in flesh and blood. For instance, when Scott writes about the hundreds of dead whales he sees on the shore. Hundreds of marine mammals, hunted and killed by whalers, now lying there like the huge wreckage of an invincible armada. I can see them, I can see them more clearly, in greater detail, than the fish I've seen just recently in the sea.

The wife of the lighthouse keeper Stevenson and Scott visit has just given birth to her first child. The two of them were so isolated from the world that she had to act as her own midwife. The keeper shows Scott the wreck of a Danish vessel, a ship that had been unable to read the lighthouse's signal in time.

Today an Italian girl named Ambra arrived at the residency. She's very pleasant. We went for a walk together along a stretch of the Camino de Santiago and then to the beach. I didn't go in because the water was freezing. I can't get used to the idea of swimming in the sea when it's cold. Ambra did take a dip.

If this were another sort of diary, there would be more personal reflections, memories of childhood visits to the seaside, of sunstroke, my mother teaching me to race the waves, and my fear when she swam far from the shore, of the gritty feel of sunblock on sandy skin and of the smell of barbecued fish.

It would also refer to Scott differently. I'd have to give my opinion on the stories he tells. Say that I like his curiosity, the way he observes people, describes them without being judgmental. Even when he says, for example, that they are ugly and superstitious, there's a level of objectivity—never disdain or condescension.

JUNE 30

Agustín took me to Luarca. There's a nineteenth-century lighthouse there, white with a prismatic base, decorative stonework, and high windows. Adjoining it is the keeper's house, which is almost the same height as the lighthouse, has a slate roof, and stands next to a marine graveyard. Agustín said that the town lies close to an oceanic trench and is famous for its giant squid. I remembered Scott and that giant sea serpent seen by his Scottish friends.

Half the port was destroyed during a spell of very rough weather. Despite the heavy fog,

I did manage to make out the lighthouse and the graveyard. In the mist, everything is a little unreal, a little remembered. The stones in the graveyard faced out to sea and as Agustín inspected them, he commented on how lucky those dead sailors were to have such a beautiful view. I recalled Valéry: "and on my tombs, asleep, the faithful sea." I thought: this is one sort of marine graveyard, but the whole sea is a cemetery, a single, enormous tomb.

I took a bus to San Sebastián. There was fog the whole way.

July 1

In San Sebastián the sky was clear and the beach carpeted in brightly colored towels. There was a small island in the center of the bay and on that green island was a tubular white lighthouse standing next to the keeper's gray house. It was noon, but the lamp of the lighthouse was lit, although barely visible, like the light of a dying firefly.

That was the first time I'd traveled to a lighthouse by ship—in fact, it was more like a motorboat than a ship. On the island, as I ascended to the tower, the path was crowded with tourists. I saw them at very close quarters: the tourists and the lighthouse.

The tourists had towels slung over their shoulders and carried flip-flops in their hands. They had bags of potato chips, beach balls, and bottles. Children were running around everywhere, crying, and it was hard to distinguish their wails from the screeching of the seagulls. Teenagers were playing "Nothing Else Matters" and reggaetón at full volume. But near the lighthouse there wasn't a single day-tripper.

The building was closed, covered in guano; its lantern lit and its windows broken.

I sat down on the quay to wait for the boat to return. Nearby, two teachers were counting a group of children in the Basque language, Euskara. One of them was missing. Another was crying about having lost his water bottle. Yet another, pointing to their teacher, said to his companion, "See? Her butt's wet." Beside me, a girl was leaning over the railing, and I said, "Look, a fish." She replied, "I like the way it pokes its mouth out. Do they need to breathe?"

On the far end of the bay of San Sebastián are the Chillida sculptures, called the *Peine del viento* (*Comb of the Wind*). There, where the waves break against the rocks, Chillida had a number of conduits cut into the stone of the quay. When the waves come in they travel up the conduits and emerge at high pressure through the openings. They look and sound like whales spouting. The sculptures on the rocks resemble hands attempting to trap the wind.

Scott's ship has difficulty in reaching the lighthouse. Eddies and currents hold it back for a long time, although it does eventually get to its destination. On the island where they weigh anchor is a hole through which the waves pass, the sound they make is exactly like the breathing of a whale.

July 4

I haven't written for days. But that sometimes happens with diaries (it doesn't happen to Scott, who writes every day without fail). People came to the Palacio and they distracted me from my task. As a diarist, I lack discipline. I'm not orderly. There are things that only occur to me afterward, things I forget, or think of later, and end by writing down at some other moment. In diary terms, that's like cheating. Although I'm not certain because, as I said before, I don't know how to write a diary. So this can't be a diary. It's nothing more than a log. I prefer it to be a log because there are fewer rules, and the diary was making me feel bad because I didn't tell everything, because I wasn't completely honest. I was troubled by not having a clear idea of what it means to be honest (Is not saying everything the same as telling a lie?), wondering if honesty has any value or what that value might be. I omit things here, but I don't know if it's to hide them or just from my desire to cut down on extraneous information. Such as what I've been thinking lately: that I don't know how to enjoy myself. Whenever I'm happiest, as is the case these days among lighthouses and people, I'm also sad. I believe I have that nostalgia for the present that Borges's character suffers from, and I don't know if there's any cure for it.

I came to a conclusion about myself that would fit very well in a diary, if this were a diary: I avoid human company because I love it. I'm capable of feeling fond of anyone with whom I've spent a certain amount of time, and then it makes me very sad to be apart from them.

I prefer not to think about these things but to recount others. Such as Scott's voyage. There are times when I find it so moving that I want to transcribe the whole book. I'd like to be a ship that carries people to the Pharos. I'd like to be the Pharos. I'd like to be more like a ship or a mirror, and less like a filter.

I should try to be more orderly in this diary or log. I should use subheadings, as Scott does, and write *Domestic Memoranda* (under this subheading Scott complains about Scottish eggs, which he claims taste earthy) when I want to talk about what a dreadful cook Pili is, and how I can't stomach one more scrap of meat. At this moment, for example, a *Nota Bene* would work well to add that there has been more than one argument between Pili and the guests at the Palacio. Pili accused us of having moved into her house without permission, and one day she left our cutlets unheated on the front steps. Now that most of the others have gone, Pili frightens me a little.

July 6

There was only one other guest left. Her name was Yolanda. She accompanied me to Cudillero, a town filled with colorful dwellings that has a yellow lighthouse beside a bungalow with a tiled roof. We tried to go up to the lighthouse, but the road had been destroyed in bad weather and it was impossible to get through.

We sat on a bench looking toward the lighthouse, talking of sad things, and I was reminded of my aunt Dolores, who is eighty and that same day had written to me about an article I'd published. She said I had a "very characteristic nostalgia." The idea that nostalgia could be something that characterizes me doesn't make me happy, so Dolores must be right.

July 7

Omission:

I didn't write anything on July 5 because there was nothing much to say. I spent it at the beach with the guests from the Palacio. But there is something I should have noted. We went to dinner at a restaurant on the highway. As night fell, I saw a number of bats and chatted with Andrés, Agustín's son, who is fourteen. He told me that the local lighthouse keeper had mentioned a green flash across the sun. The keeper had told Andrés that he'd watched every sunset for the last twenty years, and had only seen the green flash three times. According to Verne, that green flash ends all false hopes and illusions in matters of the heart. It has the gift of disillusionment. I want to see it.

July 8

Charlie, a friend of Agustín who works in the town closest to the Palacio, offered to take me cycling through the countryside. He showed me an enormous eucalyptus tree that had been planted in 1870 by an eleven-year-old named Octavio Cancio y Cuervo. We also saw the house that still contains the first chest that carried maize to Europe, and the ruins of a Celtic hill-fort. They were completely covered in scrub, but I was able to imagine what they had once been. Charlie explained how a series of hill-forts along the coast had once communicated between each other by fire signals, like lighthouses in conversation. A warbler with an orange breast suddenly alighted on the ruins.

If this were a real diary, I'd now recount how that bird reminded me of another bird I saw one day when I was saying goodbye to someone. If this were a diary, I'd recount what happened on the day I saw that other bird. But as this is a log not a diary, and as what I want to do on this journey is to forget that day, that other journey, and that farewell, I'm not going to continue. There's only one part of that story I should include here: at the end of that day, after dark, I found a postcard with the definition of the Celtic word *hiraeth*: the nostalgia for a home to which one cannot return or that never existed. I wonder

ON LIGHTHOUSES

if, during his travels through Scotland, Scott ever
heard that word. If he learned it and, when he
was aboard the *Pharos*, ever experienced that nostalgia, which is exactly what I feel now. I believe
all those fictional mariners—those Sinbads who,
once back on dry land after undergoing ordeals
immediately set sail again—know that there is no
going back. There is no way to return.

Scott's provisions are running low and his
clothes are in rags. Stevenson goes to visit a lighthouse and returns with a little butter. During
the night they spend a long time watching the
movement of the ship stirring phosphoric effects
on the water.

BIBLIOGRAPHY

The information on these pages is taken from a number of books on lighthouses, particularly *The Lighthouse Encyclopedia* by Ray Jones, (Globe Pequot Press); *Phares*, published by the Musée National de la Marine, France; *Los faros de Campeche: Guías de luz*, published by Porrúa and the Government of Campeche; *Phares & feux de Normandie* (OREP Editions) and *Le Roman des phares* (Omnibus), edited by Dominique Le Brun.

When I mention the interview with the lighthouse keeper in Puerto Escondido, I am specifically referring to one carried out by David Martín del Campo, which appears in his book *Los mares de México: Crónicas de la tercera frontera*. Another important source of the words of lighthouse keepers is a documentary film made by Ronan Glynn and Liberty Smith called *Behind the Light*.

Other quotations and references in the book can be found in the following sources: *The Seafarer*, an anonymous Anglo Saxon poem; *The Iliad*; "El faro" by Juan José Arreola; *Krapp's Last Tape* by Samuel Beckett; "Eduard Fuchs: Collector and Historian" by Walter Benjamin; *Cataract* by John Berger; "The Fog Horn" by Ray Bradbury; *Watermark* by Joseph Brodsky; *Plainwater* by Anne Carson; "Soliloquio del farero" by Luis Cernuda; *El miedo en el occidente: Siglos XIV–XVIII* by Jean Delumeau; "Farther Away" by Jonathan Franzen, published in the *New Yorker*; *Montauk* by Max Frisch; "El faro" by José Gorostiza, from the series *Dibujos sobre un puerto*; *Basenji* and *El faro por dentro* by Menchu Gutiérrez; *History of the Roman Empire since the Death of Marcus Aurelius* by Herodian; *The Sea Inside* by Philip Hoare; *Ulysses* by James Joyce; *Moby Dick* by Herman Melville; *La Mer* by Jules Michelet; Book iii, chapter iii of Montaigne's *Essays*; *El faro del fin del Hudson* by Antonio Muñoz Molina; *Natural History* by Pliny the Elder; "The Light-house" by Edgar Allan Poe; *Butes* by Pascal Quignard; *Northern Lights: Or, a Voyage in the Lighthouse Yacht to Nova Zembla*

*and the Lord Knows Where in the Summer of
1814* by Sir Walter Scott; *Records of a Family of
Engineers* by Robert Louis Stevenson; *The Twelve
Caesars* by Suetonius; *The Lighthouse at the End
of the World* by Jules Verne; "From Montauk
Point" by Walt Whitman; *Lighthousekeeping* by
Jeanette Winterson. By Virginia Woolf: *To the
Lighthouse* and *The Diaries,* except for the quota-
tion "'Twere now to die, 'twere now to be most
happy," which can be found in *Mrs. Dalloway*,
and is originally taken from *Othello*; and finally
"Grace Darling" by William Wordsworth.

ACKNOWLEDGMENTS

This collection of lighthouses is conjugated in the plural. The people around me have contributed suggestions of books, quotations, videos, and websites. They have given me lighters, magnets, clips, bookmarks, mugs, and cards with lighthouse designs, and they have sent me drawings, images from comics and cartoons. I've received postcards of lighthouses in Puerto Escondido, Isla Mujeres, Thailand, Puerto Progreso, California, Australia, Tijuana, Oregon, La Paz, Norway, Chile, and Greece. In some way, I too traveled to those lighthouses.

Thank you to all those very dear friends who read the multiple versions of this book and who have been, to quote Baudelaire on painters, "a beacon lighting a thousand citadels": Nayeli, Aurelia, César, Elisa, Jorge, Gabriela, Mariana, Verónica, Darío, Tania, Isabel, Daniel,

Marina, Astrid, Lorena, and Marie.

My thanks go to Jorge Solís for his invaluable help in editing this book and for this beautiful quotation from Eugenio Montale, which unfortunately couldn't be included in the main text: "Your restlessness makes me think / of migrant birds that fly / crash into lighthouses / on stormy nights." Also to Julián Lacalle, who gave this book a second home and presented me with the text by Antonio Cabrera that contains these words: "Lighthouses are earth raised on the earth to make the earth visible. Their lights comb the marine darkness, burdened with the true concern of man for man." And to CJ Evans for believing in this book and finding another home for it on the West Coast.

Thank you also to Antonio Muñoz Molina for his support. To Rodrigo and Huáscar for lending me their photographs and offering their friendship. To the Fundación para las Letras Mexicanas for the grant that allowed me to start to write, and to Marta Cervera and Agustín Cerezales for the residency where I finished this text. My thanks also go to Vicente Quirarte and Sergio Chejfec for their help and advice during this project. And I would also like to thank Andrea Montejo, Paula Canal, and Christina MacSweeney for taking these lighthouses on a journey to unexpected places.

And a whole world of thanks goes to Alejandro Zambra for showing me the penguin lighthouse (the most cheerful one in the world) and for so many other things. And to Silvestre: tyke and sprog.

JAZMINA BARRERA was born in Mexico City in 1988. A former fellow at the Foundation for Mexican Letters, she has a Master's Degree in Creative Writing in Spanish from NYU, which she completed with the support of a Fulbright grant. Her book of essays *Foreign Body/Cuerpo extraño* was awarded the Latin American Voices prize from Literal Publishing in 2013. Two Lines Press published her *Linea Nigra*, in translation from Christina MacSweeney. She has also published work in various print and digital media, such as *Nexos*, *Este País*, *Dossier*, *Vice*, *El Malpensante*, *Letras Libres*, and *Tierra Adentro*. A grantee of the Young Creators program at FONCA, she is editor and cofounder of Ediciones Antílope. She lives in Mexico City.

CHRISTINA MacSWEENEY received the 2016 Valle Inclán prize for her translation of Valeria Luiselli's *The Story of My Teeth*, and *Among Strange Victims* (Daniel Saldaña París) was a finalist for the 2017 Best Translated Book Award. Among the other authors she has translated are: Elvira Navarro (*A Working Woman*; *Rabbit Island*), Verónica Gerber Bicecci (*Empty Set*; *Palabras migrantes/Migrant Words*), and Julián Herbert (*Tomb Song*; *The House of the Pain of Others*).